D0212988

The Tea Party Divided

The Tea Party Divided

The Hidden Diversity of a Maturing Movement

Heath Brown

 PRAEGER™

An Imprint of ABC-CLIO, LLC

Santa Barbara, California • Denver, Colorado

Copyright © 2015 by Heath Brown

All rights reserved. No part of this publication may be reproduced, stored in a retrieval system, or transmitted, in any form or by any means, electronic, mechanical, photocopying, recording, or otherwise, except for the inclusion of brief quotations in a review, without prior permission in writing from the publisher.

Library of Congress Cataloging-in-Publication Data

Brown, Heath A.
   The Tea Party divided : the hidden diversity of a maturing movement / Heath Brown.
     pages cm
   Includes bibliographical references and index.
   ISBN 978-1-4408-3644-2 (alk. paper) — ISBN 978-1-4408-3645-9 1. Tea Party movement.
2. Conservatism—United States.   I. Title.
   JK2391.T43B77 2015
   320.520973—dc23   2015013006

ISBN: 978-1-4408-3644-2
EISBN: 978-1-4408-3645-9

19   18   17   16   15   1   2   3   4   5

This book is also available on the World Wide Web as an eBook.
Visit www.abc-clio.com for details.

Praeger
An Imprint of ABC-CLIO, LLC

ABC-CLIO, LLC
130 Cremona Drive, P.O. Box 1911
Santa Barbara, California 93116–1911

This book is printed on acid-free paper ∞

Manufactured in the United States of America

Contents

Contents

Acknowledgments

To write a book about a political issue as it is unfolding poses many challenges. Without the speedy response of other scholars working on similar issues, I would not have been able to complete the book in such a timely fashion. In particular, I thank Jonathan Mummolo, Vanessa Williamson, Devin Burghart, Stacy Ulbig, and Ronald Rapoport for sharing their research and responding to my inquiries. I appreciate the feedback on a draft of the manuscript from Glenn Feldman. I also have greatly benefited from what I've learned from the previous research on the subject, particularly the writing of Christopher Parker, Matt Barreto, Anthony DiMaggio, Christine Trost, and Theda Skocpol. I acknowledge the other scholars in the area throughout the book and in the citations. I've also talked to Tea Party activists and thank them for their willingness to speak about their work, in particular Greg Aldridge of the Roanoke Tea Party.

I also thank the institutions that helped me complete the project, including Seton Hall University, the City University of New York, John Jay College of Criminal Justice, and Steeplechase Coffee. Jessica Gribble at Praeger invited me to submit the manuscript, and I have her to thank for its ultimate publication.

My family has supported my research and this book with their own inquiries about my progress and interesting questions about the findings. And I cannot submit a manuscript on any subject without the love and support of the best editor and wife in the world, Kate Storey.

Chapter 1

What Is the Tea Party? Overview of a Maturing Movement, 2009–2014

Like many political trends, the success of thousands of grassroots volunteers, a potent blend of conservative and libertarian ideals, and a few individuals with large sacks of money owes a lot to the powerful, but often deceptive nature of naming and nostalgia. The Tea Party seized the imagination of the American public, in part, because of how it evoked one of the powerful national origin myths. Just as the American Dream animates the imagination of those on the Left, the popular fable of revolt, independence, and the quest for freedom, captured in the ceremonial dumping of chests of English tea into Boston Harbor in 1773, opened a critical vein of the American Right two hundred and fifty years later. Smelling of moth balls, Tea Party enthusiasts quickly unpacked their tri-corner hats, stockings, and powdered wigs from the long forgotten trunk of bicentennial celebrations. Outfitted and ready, thousands marched, shouted, and sung to the tune of recapturing all that was right about the country and casting off all that was now wrong. To believe in the myth of the Tea Party was to believe in the rebirth and second-coming of the American Revolution, or at least one telling of that story.[1] A revolution for the 21st century awoke a napping zeal for Americana, but also dormant fears, resentments, and anger. Tea Party protesters held signs that read: "Stop Spendin' Stop Tyranny," "We DIED for LIBERTY not for SOCIALISM," and "Don't Tread on Me."

But early Tea Party protesters were a varied bunch. While some directed their dissent at Washington, DC, in general, and espoused the ideals of Samuel Adams, Thomas Jefferson, and even Jean-Jacques Rousseau, many others aimed maliciously at the president. Rather than shouting "*Égalité!*" and "*Fraternité!*" they perseverated on "*Liberté!*" They chanted "No Obamacare," "Fire Obama," and "Obama, Where's Your Papers?" Tea Party protesters used a wicked array of slurs, epithets, and racially charged images.[2] Swastikas, animals, and nooses adorned a small, but noticeable number of protest signs. While evidence shows that most adherents to the Tea Party were not racist, sufficient numbers relied on deeply bigoted language to make race one of the defining and unavoidable characteristics of the movement. As race defined the founding of the country, perhaps this should not come as a surprise.

Eager to satiate the Tea Party appetite for a near-biblical restoration, national figures and media institutions filled the airwaves with a steady diet of rhetorical apple pie. What began as an impromptu rant, on a largely unwatched network, rapidly spread throughout radio, television, and the Internet. You would be hard-pressed to tune in to certain stations, like CNN and especially Fox News and MSNBC, without seeing a speaker from a local Tea Party group, images from a Tea Party rally, or a national Republican figure elbowing aside his or her colleagues to take up the mantle as the leader of this growing movement.[3] Hence, the Tea Party was also an opportunity for a national conversation about what conservatism and the Republican Party stood for, and also who would be in charge of deciding that in the future. This conversation started, and remained, much more varied and complex than was initially reported.

At the same time, energized by the constant stream of Tea Party information and commentary, hundreds of new groups formed, local leaders chosen, and policy agendas drafted. Despite the name, these Tea Party groups did not take the form of a traditional political party, with a tight, federated structure of national, state, and local chapters. Rather the organizations of the Tea Party resembled a scattered array of political interest groups, linked together by a loose set of ideas, rather than a formal institutional structure. These groups ranged in size from a just handful seated around kitchen tables to much more organized and increasingly sophisticated political machines of hundreds to thousands. The number of groups mushroomed quickly—estimated to be over 1,000 in just a year—but were not just found in traditional hotbeds of conservatism across the South, but also in northeastern cities, midwestern suburbs, and rural western towns. The groups that called themselves Tea Party were just as diverse in their purpose, operations, and management as the people who joined.

The Tea Party movement that started in 2009 grew rapidly, evolved, and entered into a new phase from 2011 to 2014. With this evolution or maturation comes an opportunity to better reflect on what it actually was at its founding, what it became, and what it might become in the future. Just as there are many types of tea (white, black, Oolong, Rooibos, and more), the Tea Party may best be understood as a series of Tea Parties, and, several years removed from the inception point, we now have sufficient research, evidence, and polling to better explicate the variety of meanings of the Tea Party.[4] We can think of the *Tea Partiers*: those individuals who make some claim to agreeing with the values, beliefs, and agenda of the Tea Party. Their level of devotion, priorities, and interest varies greatly and in some fascinating ways. We can also think of the *Tea Parties* what Theda Skocpol and Vanessa Williamson called "a gaggle of jostling and sometimes competing local and national organizations,"[5] since so many different types of groups formed at the local level—most with almost no formal linkage to any other groups—and several major institutions wrestled for control of the national message. And we can also start to think of the Tea Party *futures*, because there are a multitude of possible directions the movement might take. The aim of this book is to better understand the variety within the Tea Party, including the differences that exist between adherents to the Tea Party, both individuals, financial backers, and elected officials; the differences that exist between the types of Tea Party organizations; and the possible differences in what will come next for the Tea Party. These futures depend in part on those within the Tea Party, but increasingly relate to those outside, from the Republican Party, Democratic Party, and others.

THE FOUNDING OF THE TEA PARTY MOVEMENT

There are numerous explanations for what produced the Tea Party movement. Many popular accounts focus on the first notable reference to the Tea Party as a metaphor for popular opposition to President Barack Obama. Broadcast live on the floor of the Chicago Mercantile Exchange in February 2009, CNBC contributor, Rick Santelli, turned to traders and asked if they wanted to bailout those who were unable to pay their home mortgages. A chorus of "no's" prompted Santelli to face the camera and demand: "President Obama are you listening?" He then continued: "We are thinking of having a Chicago Tea Party in July" (You can view Santelli's 2009 rant at http://video.cnbc.com/gallery/?video=1039849853).

This short diatribe—which Santelli later claimed was unplanned—immediately resulted in little action. A handful of protests a week later drew small crowds and little fanfare. But momentum quickly grew as other national media outlets took up the symbolism and potential of the historic allusion to the Boston Tea Party. Santelli's rant became a frequent reference for television and radio personality, Glenn Beck, and it even resulted in a response from White House spokesman, Robert Gibbs. A general protest called for April 15, Tax Day, drew hundreds of thousands of attendees and widespread public attention, and sparked unprecedented local organizing. In interviews with early Tea Party leaders, Skocpol and Williamson discovered that most activists focused on that Tax Day rally in 2009 as the moment when they got involved for the first time. Thus, an initial explanation of the Tea Party focuses on the difficult financial politics of the late 2000s, rapidly increasingly unemployment, and a series of government policies aimed at staving off a second Great Depression, including the so-called bailouts. The confluence of these forces resulted in great economic frustration and resentment of federal policies that seemed to favor the nation's elite over the working class. What emerged a few years later on the Left in the form of the Occupy Movement first grew into the more conservative Tea Party on the Right. Thus, shortly after 2009, the founding of the Tea Party movement could be best understood as a unique time of organizational formation: drafting by-laws, writing mission statements, and deciding on which activities each group would pursue.

Rather than a bottom-up, spontaneous movement of grassroots activists and organizing, some claim that the Tea Party is largely top-down, dominated mainly by business interests. Anthony DiMaggio wrote: "The forces of corporate capitalism and the Tea Party are intertwined" and that "the rise of the Tea Party is merely the most recent chapter in a process whereby public discourse is dominated by market fundamentalist voices."[6] Matt Kibbe, the self-described Austrian school economist, and longtime Washington insider who was chosen to lead the Tea Party–linked political group, FreedomWorks, exemplifies this aspect of the Tea Party movement. This type of interpretation of the Tea Party awards little credit for the movement to protesters, voters, and local organizers, but rather sees the Tea Party as primarily effective corporate branding and Astroturf lobbying. There is merit to this view, but this interpretation also doesn't neatly explain the fact that most Tea Party groups have been tiny and raise less than a $1,000 a year to support their operations. While big money was certainly involved, the Tea Party wasn't solely a function of corporate manipulations.

Others seek to integrate these strands, and track the Tea Party movement to deeper roots and existing political institutions that help explain the speed and growth of the movement. Rather than a spontaneous and new expression of political dissent, Skocpol and Williamson suggested that three extant forces came together—a process of bottom-up and top-down politics—to form what we came to label as the Tea Party. They argued that only when looked at together does (1) the grassroots activism of hundreds of local groups, (2) national funders teamed with an eager Republican Party, and (3) powerful media outlets best explain how the Tea Party advanced so quickly from a handful of protesters to a national movement. The national Republican Party, seeking to refashion its public image after its first presidential loss in eight years, saw the public and grassroots activist enthusiasm for the Tea Party as an opportunity to update its mass appeal. While there were some Tea Party Democrats and Libertarians (both party members and ideologues), it was the Republican Party that was primed for the greatest opportunity to benefit from this flare of anger and excitement. The financial super elite, represented prominently by the Koch brothers, also saw the growing enthusiasm for the idea of a Tea Party as a way to reframe their opposition to President Obama with new populist rhetoric, appealing to working-class white voters without changing an underlying business-friendly policy agenda. With excess cash on hand, and a set of increasingly friendly campaign finance regulations for outside spending, money could be spread more widely and independently of the two major political parties. And, popular news outlets, such as Fox News and conservative talk radio, gathered a wide audience by providing adherents to the Tea Party beliefs with programming that further built support and turbocharged existing anger and frustration. These three forces made it possible for the bits and pieces of political opposition to metastasize so rapidly into a political movement.

Others have expanded on this explanation but have gone deeper. Ian Haney Lopez largely agreed with Skocpol and Williamson, but further unpacked the reasons why the charged rhetoric of the Tea Party was so effective in mobilizing certain citizens.[7] Lopez opined that supporters of the Tea Party were primarily Ronald Reagan Democrats and devotees to the 1960s' conservative (or what Doug McAdam and Karina Kloos called the "white backlash" movement) associated with Barry Goldwater.[8] Lopez argued that this alliance of mainly white and older Americans has been unified and mobilized by five decades of strategic rhetoric aimed at tying a racially antagonistic belief system to an antigovernment agenda. In this way, Lopez showed that many Tea Party movement leaders have used the same "dog whistle politics" that began in the 1960s—opting for subliminal and coded racist messaging instead of overt and transparent—in order to stoke anger and resentment at African Americans, Hispanic Americans, and others implicitly linked to federal aid programs. To play a racial dog whistle is to rhetorically substitute antigovernment hostility for anti-minority. As such, Lopez showed that the powerful emotion of anger must be understood as a simmering sentiment that Santelli, Beck, and others could bring to a boil.

And further, that this anger was not new: it has been strategically manipulated for political effect for much of the 20th century; we simply had a new and evocative way to name it after 2009: the Tea Party.

There is considerable empirical evidence to support this explanation of the Tea Party, though it is hard to disassemble Tea Party attitudes toward race, in general, from impressions of the election of President Obama, in particular.[9] Views on race, immigration, and social programs vary somewhat across the population of Tea Party supporters, but antipathy toward President Obama has almost universal agreement. Polling in October, 2010, showed that 55% of non–Tea Party Republicans "disliked Obama," versus 90% of Tea Party supporters![10] For some portion of this majority of the Tea Party, those negative feelings are closely linked with the president's race and ethnicity; Tea Party attitudes toward African Americans, in general, were substantially more resentful than for non–Tea Party Republicans. What this also suggests is, at the very least, moving the inception of the Tea Party movement to November 2008—months before the February 2009 CNBC rant—the day the country elected President Obama. Early planning and organizing of the opposition to his presidency, the first for an African American, commenced simultaneously with the counting of that 270th Electoral College vote.[11]

A related explanation for the Tea Party's emergence looks to the style of the movement. A number of commentators have linked the Tea Party to the "paranoid style" in American politics best articulated by Richard Hofstadter. Rather than a new phenomenon, or even one with its roots in the 1950s, perhaps the Tea Party connects best to the long American history of anti-intellectualism fostered by evangelical religious traditions, practical mindedness, and populism.[12] The paranoid style always sits in the soil of American politics, or perhaps even within the deep psychology of people more generally, but on occasion sprouts into populism, McCarthyism, and the movement behind the John Birch Society.[13] Robert Horwitz wrote: "The rise of the Tea Party in the wake of the economic crisis and the election of Barack Obama prompted a further revisit of Hofstadter. Some Tea Partiers' baffling pronouncements on Obama's purported non-citizenship, Islamic faith, and treasonous Kenyan socialism were seen by many as the latest display of paranoid style in American politics."[14] To accept this argument, we must think of contemporary movements as inextricably linked to previous movements, and understand the Tea Party movement as a chapter in a long history of American political development. But to place too much stock is this explanation risks emphasizing the extremes of the Tea Party, despite the fact that some scholars have opined that "the fringe does not define the [Tea Party] movement."[15]

These are all compelling explanations, but these attempts at a general theory for the Tea Party—a worthwhile ambition—may have overstated the degree of homogeneity across and within the Tea Party. For example, possibly as much as 40% of Tea Party supporters were not affiliated with the Republican Party, rather they were registered Democrats, Libertarians, or Independents. Some Tea Party organizations had million-dollar donors, but most operated on tiny budgets and the time of volunteers. And there were numerous organizations and supporters across traditional red states in southern and midwestern parts of the country, but membership grew at the nearly same rate in the mainly blue Northeast and West states. While many of the supporters were older, white, and male, several of the most important elected officials affiliated with the movement were relatively younger and nonwhite, such as Congressman Justin Amash, and Senators Ted Cruz and Marco Rubio. Prominent women, such as Congresswoman Michelle Bachman (MN) and Governor Sarah Palin (AK), were widely supported by Tea Party members and held as "folk heroes" by many.

Thus in seeking out another explanation for the Tea Party, the aim of this book is to better explain the diversity within the Tea Party. I pursue this aim, not to overturn the existing general theories described earlier, but to compliment, deepen, and add detail to how we understand this complex and maturing political phenomenon. A thorough analysis of the Tea Party can also make better sense of its importance as a type of social movement and can lead to better understanding of future social movements.

PHASES OF A POLITICAL MOVEMENT

At the publication of this book, we sit several years from the "official" start of the Tea Party movement, 2009. Because this movement scaled so rapidly, growing in numbers and also in the popular awareness, the movement matured faster than any previous political movement in U.S. history. If we compare the Tea Party movement to the civil rights, antitax, or women's movement, each of which emerged as powerful national movements capable of influencing policy and winning elections only after generations of activism, we can best appreciate this remarkable pace. It took women's organizations decades to gain suffrage rights for women and civil rights leaders a hundred years to finally gain full and protected voting rights for African Americans. The Tea Party moved much more quickly, in part, because of the deep political foundation mentioned earlier, but also the advent of new political technologies and external support. As a result, questions have been raised about the authenticity of the Tea Party as a social movement, and many may chafe at comparisons to these other remarkable movements in U.S. history. In the book, I consider these questions and the extent to which the Tea Party is truly grassroots in its nature or something else. My short answer is that the Tea Party has been both, and the duality of the Tea Party adds to what we can learn from it about social movements in general, the contemporary period in U.S. politics, and the future. Thus the Tea Party movement must be understood on those historic and contemporary terms. I argue that the Tea Party shifted from the early, infant, or first phase to the adolescent, second phase following the 2010 election. The first phase, from approximately February 2009 to November 2010, 20 months, was represented by three things: organizational formation, membership growth, and protest. These three things characterized the first phase as outsider, frenetic, and uncoordinated.

It is worth noting that I purposefully chose the term *phases* to refer to the changing Tea Party movement rather than *waves*. I made this choice for two reasons. First, the metaphor of waves has been at the center of explanations of the women's movement, but not without limitations. Kristin Goss argued that the wave metaphor has tended to limit which types of women's organizations and which issues researchers focus upon.[16] The term phases of a political movement may be less prone to this liability and better fit the Tea Party. Second, I refer to phases to distinguish my interpretation from Clarence Lo who referred to waves of the Tea Party. Lo examined waves of Tea Party protests: the first wave from February to March 2009, the second from April 15 onward.[17] He explicitly addressed the importance of protests as a defining feature of the early phase of the movement, thus breaking that time period up into waves. My approach focuses more broadly and treats these two waves as a part of the first phase that was dominated by protest politics. The second phase represents a shift from protest and organizational formation to governance and institutionalizing power.

As such, things began to change for the Tea Party following the midterm election of 2010. The Tea Party movement shifted from outsider to insider, from the periphery to the center. Tea Party voters moved from loudly protesting to patiently voting. And many were successful in supporting Tea Party candidates. Approximately 100 candidates for Congress won their campaigns in 2010. Many of these campaigns received support from sophisticated and well-funded Tea Party–affiliated organizations that lavished certain candidates with enormous amount of outside money and campaign acumen. Thus, starting in 2010, the second phase of the Tea Party movement began in earnest, now defined by actual political power in the halls of Congress, more institutionalized and mature organizations, and the opportunity to influence policy not just political debates on television. And at the end of 2014, the Tea Party may have entered into something altogether new.

Much of the existing literature has focused on the first phase, but most books were written too soon to fully address this second phase and to speculate about the future. This book aims to better understand the second phase of the Tea Party by incorporating what we know about the first phase, and closely investigating the key elements of the second phase. What changed and what does that portend for later phases in the future?

THEORETICAL LEVERS USED IN THE BOOK

There are a variety of theoretical traditions that one can draw on to analyze a maturing and evolving political movement like the Tea Party. I employ theory here as an analytical lever: helping to open doors and lift weighty concepts. Theory is useful to understanding new political phenomena because it can clarify ambiguity, point out conceptual guideposts, and draw connections to analogous circumstance. I draw primarily on three traditions to help guide this book from start to finish: behaviorialism, institutionalism, and pluralism.

First, a behavioral approach helps to draw attention to the importance of the individual; his or her beliefs and attitudes; and how those individual beliefs relate to political decisions like voting, protesting, or running for office. A behavioral approach also suggests a reliance on empirical evidence on these variables, often in the form of public opinion surveys and polling. Behaviorists have conducted numerous and highly detailed polls related to the Tea Party, though these data must be read with a keen acknowledgment of the caution raised by Glenn Feldman (2014) that "public-opinion survey data have long been known to underestimate attitudes and behaviors that fall outside of the political mainstream."[18] Finally, a behavioral orientation calls for attention to the historic literature of political behavioralists and the conclusions they have drawn in the past on the relationship between the individual and politics.

Second, though political behavioralists do not deny the existence of institutions, political institutions are not central to their worldview. To understand a complex political phenomenon such as the Tea Party, I argue that existing, emerging, and brand new institutions must be fully incorporated. Thus, I also take an institutionalist approach to explaining the Tea Party. The institutions of politics include the constitutional outlines of the democratic system in the United States; the rules for voting and political participation; and intervening institutions such as organizations, private businesses, and the media. These institutions are shaped by the behavior of individuals, but also shape behavior. They must be integrated to best understand this political movement.

Third, one way to tie these two theoretical approaches together is with the theory of pluralism. Pluralism, particularly as it has been expressed in the U.S. context, suggests that groups compete for political power in democratic marketplace. Arguably a defining characteristic of the U.S. political system, organizations have formed to represent any number of interests, and been given great leeway to advance those interests, more so than other democracies. Pluralism is not without its critics, many of whom point to how disappointing pluralism has been in U.S. politics. Groups may be free to form, but for many interests—such as for children and the poor—they have not, or not to any great extent. And, worse still, the imbalance in group resources had given moneyed interests a distinct advantage in most political debates.[19] I argue that the critique of pluralism does not render the theory invalid, rather compels scholars to add nuance and detail to their applications. If we want to understand how political phenomena such as the Tea Party work, we must pay close attention to the importance of money, resources, and influence, not just blindly accept the simple version of pluralism.

My approach to the book does not aim to integrate these theories by empirically testing a series of hypotheses. Rather, I use a more descriptive analytical approach that draws on these theories as a way to identify which questions to ask and different ways to answer those questions, both quantitative and qualitative. The descriptive nature lends itself to a wide audience of political science scholars, political practitioners, and students of politics.

ORGANIZATION OF THE BOOK

These theoretical approaches dictate the organization of the book. I seek to better explain the variations within the Tea Party in its second phase by focusing on the people of the Tea Party, the organizations of the Tea Party, and the extent to which the Tea Party has participated in the competition over policy ideas and outcomes.

CHAPTER 2—TEA PARTIES: THE MOVEMENT'S ORGANIZATIONS

Quickly, over 1,000 new nominally Tea Party organizations formed across the country. But the Tea Party did not have the federated structure of previous U.S. political movements such as the antitax movement of the 1900s or the women's movement of the early 20th century. The decentralized nature of the movement created very different types of organizations:

some for-profit corporations, others nonprofit; some aiming to mobilize members, others focused mainly on supporting candidates. This chapter aims to explain the diversity of organizational type and why understanding these distinctions helps to explain why over half of the Tea Party organizations quickly closed. Based on original interviews and archival document collection, I use a number of case studies of individual organizations to provide details and to animate the chapter for a wide audience.

CHAPTER 3—TEA PARTIERS: THE PEOPLE AND THEIR BELIEFS

Generically, the people of the Tea Party—those who self-identify as agreeing with or supporting the Tea Party—are conservative with a sprinkling of libertarianism. Early writing on the Tea Party, however, had little empirical basis to substantiate this claim. But subsequent public opinion and polling data show that while on some issues, such as immigration and health care, there is some consensus, on other issues, such as the legality of marijuana and abortion rights, there is much more disagreement. The chapter relies on newer data to better show important cleavages, particularly regional differences and gender differences among the people of the Tea Party.

CHAPTER 4—TEA PARTY PATRONS: WHO HAS SUPPORTED THE MOVEMENT?

One of the initial debates of the first phase of the Tea Party movement was whether this was mainly a grassroots or an Astroturf movement. Money has clearly mattered, and this chapter takes advantages of the passage of time to trace the changes in where money has come from and where it has gone. Some organizations have benefited handsomely from considerable funding, but most are run without any outside assistance. Tea Party candidates, too, are sometimes showered with much outside money, but others have run for office with little support. I provide several focused organizational case studies to point out the particular circumstances of individual mega-donors. Moreover, the Tea Party movement has occurred alongside major changes in campaign finance regulations, such as the *Citizens United* ruling by the Supreme Court. Finally, the Tea Party was supported by mass media. Cable news coverage catapulted the movement into public eye, but the tone of coverage differed, and changed as the movement progressed. The chapter links these changes in the nature of money, media, and politics to better understand the outside support of the Tea Party.

CHAPTER 5—TEA PARTY LEGISLATORS: EVALUATING THE CLASS OF 2010 AND BEYOND

The Tea Party movement has been distinctive for how quickly it went from a couple of protests to descriptive representation in Congress. The success of nearly 100 candidates for office in 2010 offers the chance to examine legislative behavior of Tea Party members of Congress. The chapter shows that, far from a homogeneous group, the class of 2010 was regionally diverse, and their voting was far from uniform. I use several case studies to focus attention on the particular voting of several illustrative Tea Party members. The chapter uses congressional vote scores published by major interest groups to assess the heterogeneity of voting on key conservative issues of the Tea Party class of 2010, and also whether voting patterns remained constant over time. The chapter also examines the paradox of a Tea Party incumbent, and how the Tea Party class of 2010 fared in subsequent elections.

CHAPTER 6: ANTICIPATING TEA PARTY FUTURES

The diversity of Tea Parties suggests multiple trajectories for the future of this maturing movement. This chapter looks ahead to see the possible directions for the organizations, people, and elected officials who may associate with the Tea Party in the future. I pay particular attention in this chapter to the 2016 election and the importance of several Tea Party presidential candidates, like Governor Sarah Palin and Senators Rand Paul and Marco Rubio. Not coincidentally, these three politicians represent different wings of the Tea Party movement (regionally, ideologically, and so on), and thus their rising prominence supports the central thesis of the book.

Chapter 2

Tea Parties: The Movement's Organizations

The habit of forming organizations has long been associated with the spirit of the American people.[1] Encouraged by the decentralized political roots of the country, citizens have tackled problems, big and small, through organization and collective action. The idea of the Tea Party sparked a similar impulse in citizens across the country in 2009. Within hours of the outburst on CNBC, those sympathetic with the thrust of Santelli's argument formed a national nonprofit called the Tea Party Patriots, existing advocacy organizations such as FreedomWorks repositioned their national strategy to help citizens organize at the local level, and others saw the opportunity to make money and formed new corporations including the Tea Party Nation. But citizens far from Washington, with little background in the professional practices of politics, also quickly came together to form hundreds of new organizations, many with just a few dozens of members. The Tea Party was not a single organization or even a political party exactly—with all the requisite structures and functions; rather it had under its broad ambit more than a thousand organizations with key distinctions between them in respect to type, purpose, and strategy.

But political movements are not static: they are defined by their dynamism, reliance on organizational learning, and evolving and maturing nature. As the Tea Party moved from the first phase (2009–2010) to the second phase (2010–2014), many local organizations closed, fissures formed between national organizations, and political strategies matured.

The organizations and organizational strategies of the second phase of the movement reveal much about the political and policy successes and failures of the Tea Party.

Thus, the organizational dimension of the Tea Party must be understood as profoundly American, but also as varied, uncoordinated, and complex. This chapter aims to explain some important elements of this variation. I rely on the approach of institutionalism and the particular contributions of interest groups and social movement scholars to better understand how the organizations of the Tea Party connect to previous U.S. political movements and ways citizens have been mobilized in the past. The chapter draws heavily on the excellent organizational histories and data collected by previous scholars, the personal accounts of organizational formation told by Tea Party leaders themselves, and an original analysis of Tea Party websites. Because of the importance of social media and technology to the Tea Party, how organizational websites evolved explains a lot about how the organizations changed.[2] In this chapter, I synthesize these various sources of information to describe the organizational dimension of the Tea Party. But to bring the formation of the Tea Party into focus, I begin the chapter with an excerpt of an interview with one of the leaders of a local Tea Party organization, based in Roanoke, Virginia. The interview reveals some of the early motivations and decisions made by Tea Party leaders.

THE ROANOKE TEA PARTY: A CASE STUDY

Interviewer:	"How did the Roanoke Tea Party start?"
Roanoke Tea Party Organizer, Greg Aldridge:	"The very first event here was a fairly disorganized meeting where a bunch of people just showed up to a place, and held a protest gathering . . . the first one was Tax Day 2009, that's really the birth of our group in Roanoke, and that was held on the little bridge downtown. The people speaking stood up on the bridge, and hundreds of hundreds of hundreds were everywhere."
Interviewer:	"How did you hear about the event?"
Greg Aldridge:	"I heard about it, but it started with people telling other people, emailing people, some of it was on Facebook, someone sent something to the local conservative radio station, so they did a story, saying conservatives are holding a protest on Tax Day, so probably a lot heard about it from that, people brought people. They started that at 4 o'clock and it lasted for a few hours, people cycled in and out,

there was a mass of people, probably 20% were people there for 30 minutes to an hour. Some came in early and had to leave. Others came in later or near the end, then different people came through."

Interviewer: "Was there a part of that event that started to turn into an organization?"

Greg Aldridge: "After it was over with, I was kind of impressed, made me think twice of what could come of these things. The organizers immediately started meeting as a group, a couple are still involved today, and they set up a business entity, so they could take donations. They organized a big organizational meeting at the Roanoke Civic Center, may have been the biggest meeting that has ever been held. Organizers spent their own money, and it was a very well organized meeting with various work groups . . . there were 700 or 800 people there in August of 2009."

Interviewer: "How was the organization structured?"

Greg Aldridge: "There was a meeting in spring of 2010, where they officially voted on by-laws and got all this official stuff going. And at that point there were groups voting on various things, one of the groups I was in said 'are we going to be our own group? Work in Republican politics? Which way do you want to go?' A slim majority didn't want to become involved in Republican Party, so we went on our own."

Interviewer: "Did you have conversations with Tea Party Patriots and other national organizations?"

Greg Aldridge: "Christie, who was the first [Roanoke Tea Party] president, signed up to be listed on the websites, Tea Party Patriots, but there was no enormous benefit to that. Some people found us through those websites . . . but as far as help or support from the national groups they have been nonexistent, they haven't politicked us that hard to do their initiatives, there wasn't communication or connection. I think by the time those [national] groups were organized well enough to start doing those things with member or participating groups, we had already figured out that most of those groups didn't exist to do what we were doing, they existed to co-opt what we were doing to a purpose they already had. We still communicated up the line, so if there were opportunities to do the thing we should be doing, that wasn't missed, but there wasn't much of that, they are a top down thing."

TYPES OF TEA PARTY ORGANIZATIONS: FORM, MANAGEMENT, AND STRATEGY

As the Roanoke Tea Party shows, Tea Party organizations sometimes formed out of the pent-up frustration of individuals in localities across the country. There was little evidence in Roanoke of billionaires stoking the local fires with cash donations, nor of extensive media coverage of the local rally. In Roanoke, as in many other parts of the country, local organizers relied upon social media and technology to plan events in small towns and cities. Some eventually formalized these events into new, local organizations with few connections to the national level of politics. Other Tea Party groups morphed from existing, national organizations and took on the label and certain principles of the movement. The various ways groups form says a lot about how they will ultimately act.

Organizations can be formed in a variety of types, which help describe their purpose and suggest certain things about their management and operations. We typically think of for-profit companies as one type of organization that is defined by a mission to generate money for individuals, be they owners or shareholders. We think of public organizations as another type, operated as a part of government in the interests of the general public. There are also nonprofit organizations that operate privately from government for some particular social or public purpose, but not for generating profits for private individuals. Most political organizations—whether they are called a professional association, a civic association, or an advocacy organization—are nonprofits, since they operate to support a community of interests, but there are many cases of for-profit companies participating in important aspects of politics, such as providing consulting, communications, or expert services for a fee. Even public organizations sometimes come together to gain representation as a group, such as the League of Cities, National Association of Counties, and National Association of Towns and Townships, but when they do so, the organization is almost always a nonprofit organization.

Tea Party organizations have been primarily, but not always, organized as nonprofits. In general, the social purpose of a nonprofit organization affiliated with the Tea Party ideology is to advance the ideas of liberty, smaller government, and lower taxes in the public sphere. Some of those organized as nonprofits have gained the legal designation from the Internal Revenue Service (IRS) as 501(c)(3) nonprofits. The federal government created the 501(c)(3) designation as a way to encourage the public to support charities by permitting tax-deductible donations.[3] In exchange for this incentive, and in order to prevent nonprofits from pursuing primarily political aims rather than social, the federal government placed limits on how much lobbying and explicit political advocacy is allowed to those granted the 501(c)(3) designation. Organizations with a 501(c)(3) status can do advocacy, political education, and mobilization as long as they are nonpartisan and not dedicated to advancing the passage or change of specific laws. For organizations that do not want to abide by these limits, they may opt for a 501(c)(4) status that provides no tax deductibility of donations, but does allow for more direct lobbying and explicit political action. Institutional scholars in political science, sociology, and economics, interested in how organizations make decisions, pay close attention to these distinctions, notably as they relate to the performance of for- and nonprofit-operated hospitals and schools, as well as the extent of political activity between 501(c)(3) and 501(c)(4) nonprofits.[4]

These organizational considerations were more than just the realm of bureaucratic minutiae for the Tea Party; they sparked a political fire. One of the major scandals of 2013 focused on whether the IRS granted 501(c)(3) status in a politically motivated, rather than unbiased, fashion. The accusers suggested that IRS officials, loyal to President Obama, were seeking to undermine his opposition—including Tea Party organizations—by cutting off their ability to fund-raise, and thus operate. In determining whether or not to grant the 501(c)(3) status to organizations that applied, IRS officials must judge organizational mission and operations, and grant a designation according to an unbiased reading of the regulations. The controversy centered on whether an IRS office in Cincinnati, Ohio, was following this method or unfairly breaking the rules.

After numerous investigations, including prominent hearings on Capitol Hill, only limited evidence of this improper practice was found to be happening in a systematic and politically motivated fashion. There were examples of Tea Party groups that were not awarded the 501(c)(3) status, and some evidence of the mismanagement of certain IRS offices, but the so-called targeting appeared to be merely a shortcut used by IRS processors to cut through the large quantity of applications, rather than a purposeful effort to harm the Tea Party.

Skeptics remained dubious. Notwithstanding the overwhelming evidence to the contrary, the lasting impression of political targeting and bias loosely coordinated by the White House permeated the second phase of the Tea Party movement. Some organizational leaders used this as a way to continue to mobilize support and activism. The idea of the government targeting conservative opposition corresponded neatly with the larger narrative of a tyrannical federal government hostile to citizens and citizen organizing. The IRS, in the past the embodiment of a system based on unfair taxes, also came to symbolize a political system that discouraged dissent through any means necessary. Much like that tea 250 years earlier, the IRS scandal complimented an ideology with deep roots in antitax and antistate beliefs.[5]

For others interested in organizing within the Tea Party, the nonprofit status was too limiting. There was money to be made on the movement, and the for-profit status would permit owners to generate revenue from Tea Party organizations, while at the same time advancing the cause of liberty. To be sure, for-profit and nonprofit organizations share much in common. They may be similar in size, structure, and strategy. For-profit and nonprofit hospitals, for example, both employ large numbers of well-trained doctors and nurses, save lives, and advance the health of a community. The key difference, though, is that nonprofit organizations do not have owners, and thus when they run a surplus, the money must come back to the organization, rather than to be shared with individual owners or investors. If a for-profit hospital generates a surplus, investors benefit directly, while for a nonprofit hospital, the surplus stays within the organization.

Therefore, a first distinction to consider between the types of Tea Party organizations is whether the founders opted for a for-profit or nonprofit designation (see Table 2.1). A second distinction is whether the structure chosen for the organization is highly centralized or decentralized. Some organizations have a small core of staff, few or no members, and a limited number of financial supporters. These organizations have a highly centralized structure and often rely on the large financial contributions of a handful of donors. Others are more decentralized, structured to encompass large numbers of subunits, chapters, and members. These organizations have a highly decentralized structure that takes advantage of a dispersed stream of revenue from numerous members, often spread out geographically.

The distinction between centralized and decentralized structure is not always a clear or unambiguous one. For example, a small organization at the local level may itself be highly centralized, but it may fit into a large

Table 2.1 Organizational Characteristics of Tea Party Groups

	Nonprofit	For-Profit
Decentralized	Tea Party Patriots	Patriot Action Network
	FreedomWorks	Network/ResistNet
	1776 Tea Party	Tea Party Nation
	Expected strategy: outside	*Expected strategy: outside*
Centralized	Tea Party Express	
	Expected strategy: inside	

organizational structure that is decentralized. The degree of centralization or decentralization also relates to the hierarchies in a political movement that may be defined by a central organization, often operating at the national level, with various regional, state, and local chapters or affiliates. To the extent that the center dictates what happens at the periphery, we would think of the movement as centralized, whereas if the center maintains only nominal control, and most important decisions are made autonomously at the periphery, we would call that decentralized.

For the Tea Party, there were several major national organizations and hundreds of local organizations, chapters, and affiliates. The relationship between the central leadership and the local leadership was not only an issue for categorizing the nature of the organizational structure but also a philosophical element of the movement itself. Part of the ethos of many in the Tea Party was defined by a preference for strong state's rights as opposed to a powerful federal authority. This belief bled over into the mission of many Tea Party organizations, at the national and local levels, that the movement should not mimic the faults they found in a governmental system dominated by Washington. In harkening back to the loose confederation of the original, post-1781 nation, Tea Party organizers sought to empower local leaders who could best speak for the interests of citizens. For these reasons, it is not always clear what the intended organizational structure of the movement was at its origin from what it was in actual practice, and also how intention and actuality evolved over time.

POLITICAL TACTICS: INSIDE AND OUTSIDE

These two organizational distinctions—for-profit or nonprofit status and centralized or decentralized structure—are strongly related to what organizations do: how an organization translates its mission to advance liberty, to shrink the size of government, and to oppose health care reform, into political action. There are many distinctions between the political tactics available to organizations, for-profit or nonprofit. Organizations may argue for legislative changes—what we call lobbying. Organizations may also petition the court system for judicial redress, represent clients, or submit amici curiae briefs to the U.S. Supreme Court. Organizations may opt to participate in the electoral process through mobilizing voters and supporting candidates—what we sometimes call electioneering. Scholars of interest groups, most famously Jack Walker, labelled these tactics part of an *inside strategy* to indicate that the tactics are utilized inside the institutions of government or the formal political system.[6] Conversely, organizations might also opt to mobilize citizens and members to protest and demonstrate, plan conferences to educate the public on policy issues, and sponsor speakers on important issues. Walker grouped these tactics into an *outside strategy*—or what others like Edward Walker might call a *grassroots* strategy—to suggest that they are employed at the periphery of the formal political system.[7] Inside tactics tend to be more direct and often hidden, while outside strategies are typically more open, unconventional, and the effect on policy change less precise.

Scholars of interest groups have explained some of the tendencies organizations have to use some, all, or none of these tactics. Organizations that opt for the 501(c)(3) status are restricted from substantial amounts of lobbying and from endorsing candidates, leaving a smaller array of political tactics available to them. Most outside tactics, though, are perfectly legal for 501(c)(3) nonprofits to employ. Organizations that opt for the 501(c)(4) or for-profit designation have fewer restrictions placed on political options and are thus free to lobby much more extensively, give political donations to candidates, and make candidate endorsements.

Organizations that are decentralized, strongly focused on members, and rely on member dues to support operations tend to use outside tactics. Jack Walker wrote: "A decentralized organization composed of many local or regional subunits whose staff members are involved in political and civic networks at the city and state level all over the country may seriously consider launching a national campaign of political education or grassroots mobilization."[8] An outside strategy fits with the organizational structure of the decentralized organization. Conversely, Walker also argued that "a large central staff headquartered in Washington . . . permits the group to engage in policy research if it wishes, place staff members on the advisory committees of federal agencies, and otherwise nurture the connections between the group and sympathetic public officials through an inside political strategy."[9] More recent research into organizational strategy has largely corroborated Jack Walker's argument. Edward Walker tested whether the rise of political consultants in the 1970s and 1980s changed the patterns of strategy. He found that "what remains common is that inside strategies of traditional lobbying and deploying expert knowledge continue to be favored by corporations and advocacy groups without members, by contrast, outside strategies of mass mobilization still tend to be the purview of labor unions, community orgs, and mass membership orgs."[10]

With this primer on some of the important theoretical factors inherent in institutionalism and interest group studies, I turn to the organizations of the Tea Party. I examine how Tea Party organizations grew during the first and second phases of the movement, how certain Tea Party organizations at the national level opted for the for-profit or nonprofit status, and how this related to which tactics they used.

HOW MANY TEA PARTY ORGANIZATIONS HAVE THERE BEEN?

Like many important political questions, the simplicity of the question belies the complexity of the answer. We know anecdotally that there was enormous growth in organizational formation around the Tea Party idea shortly after February 2009. But the speed of growth and the ease with which technology now permits groups to form make counting exceedingly difficult. It takes minutes, and nearly no money, to establish a social media page and name it "The Tea Party of [fill in your city or county name]." Within hours, hundreds of local users may affiliate themselves with the brand new organization's page. These users may leverage the social dimensions of the Internet to share information and ideas, agree to arrive at the steps of the state capitol on the day of a big vote, and protest loudly in support of their beliefs in personal liberty and limited government. Seeing this well-coordinated group of demonstrators, state legislators may opt to table a spending bill, fearing that the organizers will vote them out of office when they seek reelection. It is hard to argue that the modest beginnings of this group do not make it a Tea Party organization. But others interested in the Tea Party residing elsewhere may have quickly established a different social media account, be disappointed when no users joined, and never accomplished anything more than just the website. It seems reasonable to conclude that this is not a Tea Party organization, rather a website with a Tea Party name. Many organizations fall some place between these two extremes, and differentiating the point at which a group passes from simply virtual to real is hard to identify.

Moreover, other groups have no social media existence at all, but are fully organized and registered with the IRS as 501(c)(3) nonprofits. These organizations may have no virtual presence, but hold regular meetings, submit paperwork annually to the IRS, and accomplish numerous political objectives. Does this group count the same as a purely virtual social media network? It is hard to say.

Some Tea Party organizations were local only, operating within the narrow confines of a neighborhood or municipality. Other may be closely linked to national organizations, and seek to influence policy issues across the state in hundreds of policymaker arena, as well as within Congress. Should we count these organizations the same way since they both are based at the local level, or should we count them differently? Again, it is hard to know where to draw the line and precisely categorize.

Some organizations were founded and then quickly closed, while others have been sustained over several years. At what point do we stop counting an organization that has closed, particularly since many never incorporate as a 501(c)(3) nonprofit and have few tangible assets beyond the regular users of the website.

Thankfully, other scholars have taken on the hard work of counting. Theda Skocpol and Vanessa Williamson provided one of the first solid counts of the number of Tea Party organizations.[11] They rigorously verified the existence of thousands of potential candidates for counting in 2010. They reported 804 active groups with "some presence on the web" and 164 that were holding regular meetings.[12] This count, really an estimate of close to 1,000, they argued, "caught local Tea Parties at close to the peak of their spread" in the first phase of the movement.[13]

Skocpol and Williamson also reported on the geographic dispersion of Tea Party organizations. They showed that very few Tea Party groups were organized in Vermont, Delaware, and South and North Dakota. Conversely, California, Texas, and Florida each had more than 50 Tea Party organizations. And measured in per-capita terms, states like West Virginia, Montana, and Missouri had the highest concentration of Tea Party groups. In this early phase, the Tea Party was spread throughout the country, with organizational representation in a great variety of locations.

Most scholars use the Skocpol and Williamson number as a reasonable estimate of the size of the Tea Party, but it is an estimate that is bound by when the data were collected and verified. I argue that the 1,000 Tea Party organizations figure should be used as an estimate of the size during the first phase of the Tea Party movement, but that newer counts must be used to assess the second phase, starting after the election of 2010 and continuing through 2014. Because of the ease of starting and closing organizations, recounting helps track the dynamic trend line of the Tea Party movement.

To this point, Williamson, Knight, and Skocpol estimated the change in the size of the population of Tea Party organizations.[14] They tracked how many of the 824 local groups that were actively operating in November 2010, the end of the first phase, were still operating one year later—at the end of 2011. They used the activity of an organizational website and frequency of meetings as an indicator of continued operations. They found that two-thirds (68%) were still active, 276 "were no longer holding events," and 350 "were at least as active at the end of 2011 as they were at the start."[15] These findings suggest a decline in the number of local Tea Party organizations from the first to the second phase of the Tea Party movement. However, it is important to note that the ebb and flow of Tea Party organizations and activity were likely tied to election and campaign activity. The decline Williamson et al. found in 2011, an off-election year, might be the result of lower political engagement and organizational activity overall, not a decline in enthusiasm for the Tea Party itself.

In order to investigate this, others have continued to count the number of Tea Party organizations after the 2011 off-election year, though with slightly different methods. Scholars at the Institute for Research and Education on Human Rights (IREHR) provided one such count. In the summer of 2013, also an off-year election, IREHR conducted a survey, which "provides an unvarnished, non-partisan, data-driven analysis of the membership of the national factions as the movement approaches its sixth year."[16] While the method used to count by IREHR may be slightly different from the one used by Skocpol and Williamson, who focused on local organizations, IREHR reached a remarkably similar count of 1,072. Also similar to the earlier count, and not surprisingly given their overall size, California (93), Texas (85), and Florida (69) had the largest number of Tea Party organizations affiliated with the major national organizations. Delaware (3), the Dakotas (5 total), and Vermont (3) remained nearly free of any Tea Party organizations. Thus, from a national organizational standpoint, the number and regional composition of the Tea Party remained similar from the first to the second phase; the steep growth curve flattened quickly.

WHAT ARE THE CHARACTERISTICS OF TEA PARTY ORGANIZATIONS?

Another feature of the Tea Party that we have learned about from excellent survey research is the varied nature of those approximately 1,000 local organizations. The *Washington Post* canvassed Tea Party organizations in 2010.[17] It conducted nearly 650 interviews in the fall of 2010, in the weeks leading up to the important 2010 midterm election. It collected information from organizations and individuals from all but one state. As the *Washington Post* acknowledged when it published the findings from the survey, there are no comprehensive lists of Tea Party organizations, so the results of its research are educated estimates, not the result of a full census.

From the *Washington Post* survey we know that there was a skewed distribution of membership size in local organizations. About half of the respondents (51%) had fewer than 50 members, what most would consider small organizations. The remaining organizations had greater than 50 members, but only 39 had greater than 100 members, what we might call large organizations. Thus, there was no average local Tea Party organization: the distribution of members was non-normally distributed, with a few large outliers, but most small. It is clear from this survey research that there was great difference within the population of local Tea Party organizations.

What made Tea Party organizations similar, however, seems to be the way they funded their operations. According to the *Washington Post* research, 95% of the money organizations raised by those surveyed came from individuals, and 95% of the funds came from local sources. This finding suggests that the argument that the Tea Party was primarily an Astroturf movement, supported by a small number of elite sources, is largely untrue for most Tea Party organizations. It may be the case for a few of the national organizations described later in this chapter, but for the vast majority of small, local organizations, the way they funded operations would be best described as grassroots, member-based, and decentralized.

Moreover, the links between local and national organizations were more limited than indicative of a primarily Astroturf movement. The *Washington Post* survey showed that more than a third (35%) of local groups that responded to the survey did not work with any national organization. The survey also found that a third (32%) of local groups collaborated with the Tea Party Patriots, the national organization described in greater detail later in this chapter. A small percentage (4%) worked with FreedomWorks and other national organizations. Additionally, only 10% of the respondents claimed to make decisions "mainly or entirely" in coordination with national organizations. A majority (51%) made decisions "entirely at the local level."

Other empirical research corroborates these findings. Virgil Ian Stanford examined the content of local Tea Party websites. A centrally managed and coordinated movement would likely see local organizations providing similar content, acting merely as a funnel for messages developed elsewhere. But Stanford found that the typical website "is only likely to have about 18% of its content be the same as any other randomly selected website."[18] Stanford concluded that this lack of unity might limit the effectiveness of the movement at the national level, but is also an indication of decentralized, rather than coordinated messaging.

Other researchers largely agree with these conclusions about the first phase of the movement. Wendy Tam Cho, James Gimpel, and Daron Shaw attested to the grassroots nature of the movement by examining the geography of Tea Party protests.[19] They found little connection between the location of Tea Party events and the electoral priorities of the Republican Party. If the Grand Old Party (GOP) was manipulating Tea Party activists, one would expect Tea Party events to correspond with the strategies of electing more Republican members to Congress, but the Tea Party strategy did not overlap. Instead, Tea Party protests were concentrated in Nevada, Florida, Arizona, and California, states with the highest housing foreclosures, perhaps a nod to Rick Santelli. The authors concluded: "But while we are convinced that elites of some stripe were critical in helping to organize events, it is very difficult to see the hand of traditional, political elites in the Tea Party patterns."[20]

The tactics used by most local organizations were also what we would expect based on previous research on advocacy organizations. Most local organizations seemed to focus on organizing, local mobilizing, and planning protests, all outsider tactics. Few local organizations were directly involved in insider tactics, particularly electoral activities. Jeffrey Berry et al. found that very few local organizations endorsed candidates for elected office, an insider tactic that some national organizations pursued.[21] The nonprofit and informal status of many of the local organizations made other insider tactics such as direct lobbying, giving campaign donations, and influencing executive decision unfeasible options. The Tea Party Patriots, described in detail later in this chapter, exemplifies the outsider approach taken by many local organizations.

But it is important to recall that the *Washington Post* survey, at least, was conducted during the first phase of the Tea Party movement. It is unclear whether the high level of local control and weak links to national organizations persisted into the second (a subject I return to throughout the remainder of the book). What does seem clear is that what defined the first phase of the Tea Party movement, 2009–2010, a dynamic period of organizational formation, was not a defining feature of the second phase, from 2010 to 2014. Organizations seemed to maintain their operations, but the steep rate of growth slowed from 2011 to 2014. However, this does not mean that there was no change or that the second phase of the movement had no important local organizational component. There were some Tea Parties that closed, and others that opened, resulting in no net change in the overall count, but change nonetheless. There was also change in the size of membership in these organizations; some grew greatly and others remained the same or contracted. I return to address the defining characteristic of the second phase of the Tea Party later in this chapter, after I introduce several of the important national Tea Party organizations.

NATIONAL TEA PARTY ORGANIZATIONS

At the same time hundreds of local organizations formed in cities and towns across the country, in centers of politics—including in Atlanta, Georgia, and Washington, D.C.—political professionals and experienced activists quickly saw the potential for a national movement around the same idea of a Tea Party. For some, this meant forming new national organizations, while for others it meant transforming existing organizations into something strongly connected to the Tea Party. Some chose the nonprofit status and others the for-profit. Some were strongly connected to the Republican Party and major conservative donors; others remained purposefully distant from the two-party system and the elite politics of big money. This section aims to explain the similarities and differences between these organizations, and how their operations and significance shifted from the first to the second phase of the Tea Party movement.

TEA PARTY PATRIOTS

The first national Tea Party organization to consider is the Tea Party Patriots (TPP). TPP is significant because, while it has had a national reach, it embodied many of the strategies, tactics, and patterns of local organizations across the country. For that reason, we can learn a lot about the details of what was occurring in many different communities through the work of the TPP. We can also see the changes that occurred as we move from the first to the second phase of the movement.

TPP was incorporated in Woodstock, Georgia, as a 501(c)(4) nonprofit organization, by Mark Meckler and Jenny Beth Martin. Led by Meckler and Martin, the TPP has used a primarily outsider strategy through much of its history. In its first report to the IRS they wrote: "The Patriots supported and organized numerous events and rallies, including over 850 Tax Day Tea Parties on April 15, 2010, co-organized the March on DC on September 12, 2009 that included approximately 1.7 million participants that convened on the National Mall."[22]

One of the most important elements of executing outside tactics for the TPP was its use of the Internet. During the first half of the 2000s, progressive and liberal organizations, such as MoveOn.Org, had gained an advantage in the most sophisticated ways to utilize technology to mobilize supporters. The Tea Party represented a break in this trend. Certain Tea Party organizations "adopted different online practices" according to Dave Karpf, and showed the ways conservatives and those outside of the circle of progressive organizations could find novel ways to use the Internet.[23]

TPP was founded by leaders who brought this new expertise. In the memoir of the founding of TPP, Martin wrote: "Because I had been very active on Facebook, Twitter, and other social media, it was easy for me to quickly put up a Facebook page for an event in Atlanta."[24] The web and the various technologies related to social networks lent themselves to the organizing purpose of the TPP. Martin argued "But without Twitter, those of us who had heard Santelli's rant and agreed that it was time for a change might never have been able to come together to take action. The first American Revolution may have begun with a gunshot, but the second American Revolution began with a hashtag (a label or keyword attached to a message posted on Twitter and other social media applications to allow readers to easily search)."[25] Martin had been using the *hashtag* #TCOT (an acronym for Top Conservatives on Twitter) since President Obama's electoral victory in November 2008, to begin organizing disgruntled voters. Six months later, it was the registering of their website that the founders of TPP credit with what "formalized" their group.[26]

Because of the importance of the Internet to TPP, the structure and focus of the organization can be observed by examining the earliest iteration of the website: http://teapartypatriots.org. Political science and communications scholars have increasingly used qualitative methods to analyze and learn from public websites. For example, Jennifer Stromer-Galley tracked the use of the web in presidential campaigns from 1996 to 2012, and Melissa Merry examined the web strategies of environmental interest groups.[27] I approach Tea Party websites in a similar fashion. To start, the TPP website from February 2009 showed the hurried and somewhat amateur formation of the organization. The original TPP logo that appeared in the upper left-hand corner of the page was a portion of an image of the U.S. flag dangling above its fuzzy mirror image. The logo was basic and unsophisticated. The use of the red, white, and blue color scheme, a near-universal norm of American political campaigns, candidates, and movements, dominated the logo and website. In retrospect, the original logo of the TPP appears unprofessional and improvised, perhaps attesting to how quickly it must have been designed. Much of the early website lacked the look and feel of more professional political organizations, and certainly of later iterations of the entire TPP website.

Second, the initial, very simple site allowed users to create and log in to their own account, add a local Tea Party organization and event, and "Share Your Tea Party Experience." One of the earliest posts, written on April 16, 2009, by Rob Gaudet, contained a statement about the organization's mission that further reflected this decentralized and membership focus: "The TPP are a completely non-partisan, spontaneous movement made up of hundreds of thousands of patriots from all around the nation." The post went on to explain that "this movement has no single leader. This movement has millions of leaders. . . . This is a true grassroots movement, and the direction, message, and methodology of this movement are driven from the ground up." The post drew attention to the April 15 protests where "TPP of America assembled in over 700 cities, creating the single largest multi-city protest in American history." The earliest iteration of the website attests to the original thrust of TPP and its distinct focus on organizational process rather than political outcomes, and on outside rather than inside tactics. The founders later explained that "we were organizing the Tea Party movement along the lines of an open-source community. . . . Through this open-source feedback loop, the core of the Tea Party movement matured."

Just a few weeks later, as the organization progressed, the website had advanced and grown more sophisticated, but the structure was still decentralized and member-focused. In May, the website added a calendar, social networking feature, feedback survey, and "Idea Board." The newly designed site included links to biographical information about the founding team of Amy Kremer, Mark Meckler, Jenny Beth Martin, and Rob Neppell, as well as a new statement under the TPP logo that drew attention to how the site would help registered users "use this site to easily organize your July 4th Tea Party." The obvious focus of this statement, and thus of TPP, was on organizing protests. The calendar contained events in cities across the country, including a May 1 "May Day! May Day!" event in Pasadena, California, a May 30 "Constitution Day Party" at Gypsy Hill Park in Staunton, Virginia, and a couple dozen of July 4 events. The early version of the Tea Party "Ideas" section of the website included links for July 4 Ideas, Legislation and Constitutional Amendments, Media & Public Relations Goals, and Technology/Website. Interestingly, while Strategy & Goals had 56 comments and July 4 Ideas had 21 comments; there was only a single post for Legislation & Constitutional Amendments.

By June, the website changed again. Gone were many of the previous tabs, and now the website included links to "Patriot Feed," a running scroll of user posts, a Google Group, and Team Wiki. TPP slowly added these new technologies to expand the social networking connections that are so useful for organizing and connecting citizens. But at the same time, the new site removed the statement about helping to organize for July 4, leaving just the logo and "Official Grassroots American Movement" across the top of the site. For the first time, however, the website began to list all of the registered affiliates of the TPP: Bowling Green Tea Party Patriots, Stockton Tea Party Patriots; Humboldt Tea Party Patriots. A month later, July 26, the number of organizations listed grew to 56. And by October, there were already 84 organizations listed on the website, for California alone. We can see evidence of the remarkable level of organizational formation from these data (see Figure 2.1). This is not a precise count, as TPP likely did not verify the existence of each organization, but these figures do attest to the rapid growth in an astoundingly short amount of time: from less than 100 to nearly 1,000 in less than six months. One could argue that there has never been a period as active in organizational formation in U.S. history before and since.

Another change that emerged over the summer of 2009 revealed how TPP funded its operations. These additions to the website also demonstrated how the TPP quickly began to professionalize its operations, institutionalize its funding mechanisms, and grow. In late July, the website added a new tab "Donate to Tea Party Patriots" with a link to the online

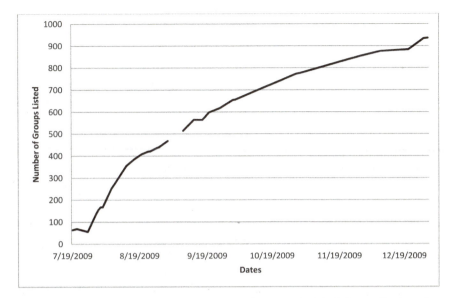

Figure 2.1 Number of TPP Groups, July–December 2009 (original data collection of archived TPP websites)

PayPal payment system. In the archived version of the website from June 27, the TPP also added a set of TPP Sponsors, including American Liberty Alliance, FreedomWorks, and Tea Party Express. By August, additional sponsors were added, including conservative commentators, Michele Malkin, RedState, and Red County, but the Tea Party Express was gone. At nearly the same point, the Tea Party Express website no longer listed the TPP as a partner on its national bus tour. The break between these two groups centered on the participation of TPP founder, Amy Kremer, in the activities of the Tea Party Express, and allegations that she sought to claim ownership over the intellectual property of TPP assets.[28] The break with Kremer ran to the heart of the philosophical and organizational differences between the grassroots orientation of TPP and the top-down style of the Tea Party Express (discussed later in this chapter).

Using changes in the website, we can also see the increasing importance of the upcoming election. TPP began to shift its focus from organizing protests and helping citizens form local organizations to influencing the election. Near the end of June, the site added a tab for "Members Up for Reelection in 2010," indicating a move from political organizing to electoral mobilization. That new section was simply an MS Excel spreadsheet with a contact list for every member of Congress, but showed an expansion of purpose and tactics. These changes from the early protest and organizational focus of the TPP to an increasingly professional and policy orientation mirror the larger shift and maturation of the Tea Party movement from the first to the second phase.

A year later, in 2010, toward the end of the first phase of the Tea Party movement, the TPP website revealed much about the growing professionalism, sophistication, and orientation of the movement. The website in November 2010 had a new, sleek logo of a shield with the stars and stripes strewn across it. The organization's mission statement was now clear and specific: "Our mission is to attract, educate, organize, and mobilize our fellow citizens to secure public policy consistent with our three core values of Fiscal Responsibility, Constitutionally Limited Government and Free Markets."[29] Gone was the MS Excel spreadsheet, replaced with a searchable database of candidates.

Four years later, in 2014, the website continued to be a source of interesting information about the structure of the TPP. Under the section, "Upcoming Events," though, there weren't any listed. Compare this to the early founding of TPP when the focus of nearly all of their activities was helping to plan and publicize protest events and rallies. Instead, the new site had detailed policy statements and links to pending bills in Congress. TPP morphed from a decentralized umbrella organization focused on outside tactics and organizing to one pursuing an increasingly inside strategy in the second phase.

FREEDOMWORKS

The story of FreedomWorks differed in many ways from that of TPP. FreedomWorks existed long before 2009 as a 501(c)(4) nonprofit organization. From its website in 2004, the mission statement explained: "FreedomWorks is a non-profit organization that fights for lower taxes, less government and economic freedom. FreedomWorks unites the nation's leading advocates of freedom with the power of hundreds of thousands of volunteer members from across the country."[30] The website highlighted the organization's "Freedom Agenda," including a push for fundamental tax reform, ending lawsuit abuse, workfare over welfare, school choice, and privacy. Other issues addressed government spending, health care reform, and international trade. The pre-2009 website demonstrated the Washington-dominated focus with links to the three chairmen: Dick Armey, Jack Kemp, and C. Boydon Gray, as well as senior fellow, Bill Bennett, each seasoned Washington political figures. The FreedomWorks of the mid-2000s was a major part of the establishment and strongly connected to the Republican Party.

What was remarkable about FreedomWorks was how quickly its leaders caught on to the potential of the Tea Party and adapted—at least rhetorically—a decentralized approach to mobilizing members and supporters across the country. On its website blog, Thomas Keeley posted the Santelli video on February 19, 2009, almost immediately after it was telecast. Keeley wrote: "Here is a great video from CNBC correspondent, Rick Santelli, on the floor of the Chicago Mercantile Exchange summarizing what I think is the sentiment of many Americans right now." A day later, Brendan Steinhauser posted on the blog "10 easy steps to organizing your own 'Tea Party' protest." Four days later, on February 24, Steinhauser posted information about a "Taxpayer Tea Party" in Bowditch Point Park in Fort Myers, Florida, on February 27. By February 26, a photo of Rick Santelli was featured on the front page of the website along with the question, "Are you with Rick? We are." FreedomWorks quickly launched a companion website, IamWithRick.Com, and wrote that they were "helping to organize other tea party protests in cities around the country." It claimed that "Nancy Pelosi, Harry Reid, and the new Obama Administration are running the bailout train full steam ahead toward the destruction of our American capitalist system and ultimately outright socialism. They must be stopped!" Despite its history and Washington, D.C., home, the organizing and protesting features of the Tea Party immediately drove Freedom-Works toward the movement.

The speed with which FreedomWorks responded to the Tea Party idea was similar to TPP, but the structure and tactics it used were different. Whereas TPP was strongly focused on the local level of politics and aimed to foment organizational formation, FreedomWorks focused much more on national-level organizing and policy advocacy. It reflected their Washington roots and strong base of financial and nonfinancial resources with a mix of inside and outside strategies.

But rhetorically, leaders of FreedomWorks emphasized the popular dimensions of the Tea Party. In the *Wall Street Journal*, two of the organizations leaders, Dick Armey and Matt Kibbe, wrote: "The tea party movement has blossomed into a powerful social phenomenon because it is leaderless—not directed by any one mind, political party or parochial agenda."[31] They continued: "Decentralization, not top-down hierarchy, is the best way to maximize the contributions of people and their personal knowledge. Let the leaders be the activists who have the best knowledge of local personalities and issues." There is a certain irony to these claims made by the president and executive director of one of the major national Tea Party organizations. If the movement was truly leaderless, Armey and Kibbe likely would not have been given the opportunity to express their views in such an august newspaper. So, how might we judge the sincerity of these claims? FreedomWorks provided ample resources to help organize, but how much control did they cede to local level of the Tea Party?

Compared to TPP, the strong connection to Washington, D.C., reliance on a staff of former Republican elected officials and staffers, and ample financial resources, suggested that FreedomWorks perspective on local organization was at the very least different.

TEA PARTY EXPRESS

Much clearer than the differences between TPP and FreedomWorks was the notably centralized approach taken by the Tea Party Express (TPE). Compared to TPP and, to a great extent, FreedomWorks, TPE was much less focused on the organizational dimensions of the Tea Party, and despite all carrying the 501(c)(4) designation, TPE was the most aggressively focused on electoral activities. Rather than organizing, protesting, and employing mainly outside tactics, TPE used insider tactics and targeted campaigns, especially vulnerable Democrats for the U.S. House and Senate. It was later aided by an election committee that could give campaign donations, Our Country Deserves Better Political Action Committee. Nonprofit organizations are permitted to form associated, but legally separated, political action committees (PACs), which can give campaign donations. The two organizations, TPE and Our Country Deserves Better PAC, could together influence election outcomes by rallying voters through the 501(c)(4) and legally supporting and opposing candidates through the PAC in ways that a 501(c)(3) nonprofit could not on its own, or at least not until the Supreme Court ruled on campaign finance reform, a subject I return to in Chapter 4.

Evidence of this approach could be seen on the original TPE website. TPE explained the bus tour they planned during the summer of 2009: "At each stop the tour will highlight some of the worst offenders in Congress who have voted for higher spending, higher taxes, and government intervention in the lives of American families and businesses. These Members of Congress have infringed upon the freedom of the individual in this great nation, and its [sic] time for us to say: 'Enough is Enough!'"[32] The most prominent tab on the website was for "Target Races." In 2009, it targeted Senator Barbara Boxer (CA), Senator Harry Reid (NV), and lesser-known members of the House, such as Dana Titus (CA), Ann Kirkpatrick, and Ciro Rodriguez (TX). TPE listed a political vulnerability for each incumbent that indicated the slim margin of victory in previous elections or recent polls. It wrote: "In order for the Tea Party movement to truly have an impact, we must vote out of office those politicians who have betrayed their constituents by pushing through massive deficits, higher taxes and government intervention into the private sector and private lives of American families. The following members of Congress are the first-wave of politicians we will be targeting. In addition to highlighting their atrocious, inexcusable conduct while in office, we will also be launching television and radio ad campaigns against these incumbent politicians." The TPE website did contain options to join an e-mail list and participate in social media, but there was little obvious effort focused on these dimensions of the organization. This seemed to reflect the orientation away from helping to form chapters, grow a membership, or mobilize other Tea Party organizations, in favor of primarily electoral objectives and an inside strategy.

A year later, in October, 2010, TPE had not changed much on their website, but did add an extensive list of "Endorsed Candidates." As a 501(c)(4), TPE maintained the ability to endorse candidates in ways that other 501(c)(3) nonprofit Tea Party organizations could not and TPP chose not. The TPE endorsed Sharon Angle in Nevada (NV), Dino Rossi in Washington (WA), Carly Fiorina in California (CA), who all eventually lost. But it also endorsed Senate-candidate Mike Lee in Utah (UT), and in House races Raul Labrador in Idaho (ID) and Jason Chaffetz in Utah (UT), who all won and soon became the heart of the Tea Party members in Congress (the subject of Chapter 5).

TPE also started to note who had donated money to the PAC. They listed dozens of $100, $150, and $200 donors who helped pay for radio advertisements in support of Sharon Angle in her race against Nevada senator and majority leader, Harry Reid. TPE raised money in small allotments, but also in much larger from significant supporters of the Tea Party (the focus of Chapter 4 of this book). Because of the nonprofit status, TPE were not required to disclose the names of all their donors.

TPE used the money raised to become an important sources of outside campaign funding in the 2010 (and to a lesser extent in the 2012 and 2014 elections), but most of the funds were not given directly to candidates. In 2010, TPE (and Our Country Deserves Better PAC) spent more than $7.7 million. In 2012, they spent nearly $2 million more, totaling $9.3 million.

Most of the money spent by TPE went for fund-raising and independent political advertisements. In 2010, for example, they paid $668,948 to Russo Marsh & Associates, the political consulting firm owned by one of the TPE founders, Sal Russo.[33] It also paid $234,151 to Fox Business Network and $120,545 to Fox News Channel for various media services to promote the organization, its events, and its issues. In 2010, TPE spent over a $1 million on media, $1 million on administrative costs, and $1 million on fund-raising. In 2012, the expenditures for TPE shifted to almost exclusively fund-raising. Fund-raising expenditures totaled nearly $7 million of the $9.3 million in total expenditures.

Interestingly, TPE donated very little to candidates directly. In 2010, for example, TPE donated a total of $16,250 to House candidates, including

$2,000 each to Michelle Bachmann (MN), Charles Djou (HI), and Michael Peter Fallon (CO), and $2,500 to Raul Labrador (ID). TPE donated more to Senate candidates, $20,500 in total, including $2,500 to Marco Rubio (FL) and $1,000 to Scott Brown (MA). Rubio and Brown both won their Senate races, but the rest, including Sharon Angle (NV), Joe Miller (AK), and Christine O'Donnell (DE), all lost.

Despite financially supporting many losing candidates in 2010, credit for some of the House and Senate victories must be tied to the massive amounts TPE spent on issue advertising. In 2012, there was a change in the pattern of campaign spending by TPE. The move from the first to the second phase of the Tea Party movement saw TPE increase its overall campaign expenditures by 17%, but its direct donations to House and Senate candidates increased by 90% and 75%, respectively. Also, TPE decreased its independent expenditures on communications and media. In 2010, TPE paid $2.7 million for independent expenditures, including more than $600,000 on the unsuccessful efforts to support Sharon Angle and Joe Miller, but in 2012 they cut that independent spending to $680,937, nearly a 300% decrease. These shifts in the composition of campaign expenditures were a part of the changing strategy of TPE as the most significant Tea Party organization primarily devoted to electioneering. TPE maintained a centralized structure and an inside strategy, even as it evolved as an organization and adjusted the way it employed campaign cash.

TPE was not without its own internal controversy. One of its early leaders, Mark Williams, had made a career as a talk-show host. His virulently anti-Obama rhetoric ultimately led to his undoing. Williams called the president a Nazi, an Indonesian Muslim, and a welfare fraud. Williams ultimately had to resign as chairman of the TPE.[34] Much as with any new organization, TPE and many Tea Party organizations confronted these internal conflicts that, in an age of social media, often spilled into the public realm. For some organizations, these conflicts hampered their activities, but for TPE, the organization continued to pursue its insider strategy through the second phase of the Tea Party movement.

PATRIOT ACTION NETWORK

Perhaps the most confusing national Tea Party organization was Patriot Action Network (PAN), previously called ResistNet, but also operated by Grassfire Nation, a division of Grassroots Action, Inc. PAN also differed greatly from the approach of TPP and FreedomWorks, but also from TPE. The founders of PAN, and also Tea Party Nation, opted to form as for-profit corporations, rather than the more typical nonprofit organization. Similar to FreedomWorks, PAN operated prior to 2009, but it was during the up-swing in attention to the idea of Tea Party that the organization took off.

The chief strategy employed by Steve Elliot, the owner of PAN, shared much in common with the outsider strategy of TPP: PAN aimed to use outside tactics to build an online community of Tea Party supporters and support protests. PAN simply went about organizing with the twin goals of advancing the political ideas of the Tea Party and generating profits for the organization's parent company.

Much like TPP, PAN was largely a virtual organization, with few paid staff and little physical infrastructure. The organization's large website, and associated multimedia social networking appendages, represented the best estimation of how the organization operated during the first and second phases of the Tea Party movement. While the organization had been in operations prior to 2009, the earliest archived version of PAN's website (www.patriotactionnetwork.com) can be found for December 2010. The site functioned as a social networking tool, much like Facebook or earlier online communities of that era, like Myspace. The main screen welcomed viewers:

Are you tired of the size, scope, and reach of the government? If so, then you have come to the right place! Patriot Action Network (formerly ResistNet) is the nation's largest conservative social action network, serving tens of thousands of citizens. . . . We invite you to sign up to get your own Patriot Action Home Page and then click here to get started.[35]

The social network website was a mix of political propaganda, calls to action, and commerce. There were sections of the site for "Latest News," "Forum," and "Groups." Each link appeared to provide a way for users to share information about the Tea Party, including events, newly formed organizations, and petitions.

It is harder to discern how PAN generated revenue from the social network website, and because PAN was not incorporated as a nonprofit, it did not report detailed expenditure and revenue data to the IRS. In a Frequently Asked Questions (FAQs), section, PAN vaguely explained: "ResistNet is operated by Grassroots Action. We will provide opportunities for those who want to financially support this website." Despite its for-profit status, PAN did solicit donations from users, by stating on its website, "Your contribution will help the Patriot Action Network engage Patriots to restore liberty and limited government!" but cautioned contributors that "Payments to Grassfire Nation are not tax deductible." The decision to incorporate as a for-profit corporation limited fund-raising opportunities for PAN.

From the main page of the website, one can see other ways that money was made. On the website in 2010, there was a cacophony of opportunities to spend money and numerous commercial links. PAN provided links along the right side of the page to buy books published by conservative authors such as Glenn Beck, Sarah Palin, and Michele Malkin. There was also a prominent button for "STORES" that linked to a "Tea Party Store Amazon" and "ResistNet Café Press" where T-shirt and other items could be purchased. The early website contained banner advertisements with links to other websites that sold political paraphernalia: "Get your Flip Stuff Now and Preserve a Piece. Flip This House Gear Is Now 50% Off!" Each of these commercial links could have generated revenue for PAN. Unlike the websites for TPE, TPP, and FreedomWorks, which were dedicated almost entirely to politics, organizing, and donations, the PAN website had a strong orientation toward marketing, and interspersed politics with commerce.

TEA PARTY NATION

For the other major for-profit Tea Party organization, Tea Party Nation, the commercial side of the organization caused problems with others in the movement like PAN. Tea Party Nation was also established as a for-profit company, and sought to advance the interests of the Tea Party through convening major events, highlighted by paid speakers from the leadership of the Tea Party. This approach rubbed other leaders the wrong way. TPP discouraged its members from attending a February 2010 convention in Tennessee organized by Tea Party Nation because of the high cost of attendance.[36] Tea Party Nation, the lead organizer of the convention, charged attendees $549 and another $349 to attend the keynote address delivered by Sarah Palin.

Though the outside strategy of Tea Party Nation and PAN, and importance of social networking made them similar to TPP, and many of TPP's local nonprofit chapters and affiliates, the decision to incorporate as businesses weakened the connections between these organizations. Generating profits from Tea Party supporters, and orienting mobilization around commercialism, disrupted the unity and consensus that characterized the earliest points of the Tea Party movement.

1776 TEA PARTY

The final significant national organization, 1776 Tea Party, similar in many ways to the nonprofit Tea Parties, strained the unity and wide acceptance of the Tea Party movement in another way. At its center, the idea of the Tea Party had been about outside strategies—disruption and immoderate tactics—and beliefs. Like other revolutionary movements, the Tea Party attracted many supporters who were disenchanted with the status quo and the moderate positions of the two major political parties in the country. But 1776 Tea Party drew those with the most unconventional beliefs and supported a level of vitriol that many other organizations in the movement, and conservative leaders outside the movement, could not condone.

From the start, 1776 Tea Party was the least coherent of the national organizations, best known for registering the Internet URL teaparty.org, first. The organization, founded by Dale Robertson, had a sparse website with few ways for viewers to get involved. One of the main tactics the organization employed was what it deemed a "Candidate registration." In order to become a member of the Tea Party, a candidate for office had to pay a one-time fee and sign on to a set of "non-negotiable core beliefs." If elected, the Tea Party anointed official would "install, protect, and endorse" the belief that:

- Illegal Aliens Are Illegal,
- Pro-Domestic Employment Is Indispensable,
- Stronger Military Is Essential,
- Gun Ownership Is Sacred,
- Government Must Be Downsized, National Budget Must Be Balanced, Deficit Spending Will End,
- Bail-out And Stimulus Plans Are Illegal,
- Political Offices Available To Average Citizens and Intrusive Government Stopped,
- English Only Is Required and Traditional Family Values Are Encouraged,
- Common Sense Constitutional Conservative Self-Governance is our mode of operation.

The pledge contained several other related promises, but the website did not make clear how many candidates signed up and paid the fee, if any did at all.

The tone of the 1776 Tea Party was what set it apart from other national organizations. The National Association for the Advancement of Colored People (NAACP), a frequent critic of much of the Tea Party movement, explained that the 1776 Tea Party "has adopted a deliberately confrontational posture."[37] Most inflammatory were the actions of Dale Robertson who carried a sign at a rally in 2009 that linked Congress with slave owners, sent a fund-raising letter with a photograph of the president dressed as a pimp, and promoted allegations about the president's place of birth.[38] While other factions in the movement—notably FreedomWorks and the TPP—disavowed the 1776 Tea Party and its leader, other organizations, such as the anti-immigration Minuteman Project, collaborated closely.

It should be clear by this point that there is no single Tea Party organization, either at the local or national level. These organizations varied so greatly in terms of structure, beliefs, and strategy—what Skocpol and Williamson referred to as the "panoply" of Tea Party organizations—that to even suggest they all fall under the same umbrella seems like a stretch. But the idea of the Tea Party, conveniently mythical in its origin, benefited from flexibility and ambiguity. Those characteristics allowed for a wide variety of activists to seize on the idea and the organizational opportunities it presented. The wide array of organizations that rapidly grew in 2009 was a testament to the fertility of the Tea Party idea.

NATIONAL TEA PARTY ORGANIZATIONS BY THE NUMBERS: FIRST AND SECOND PHASE

Some of these national Tea Party organizations provided the umbrella under which significant local organizing occurred. In fact, this was a key feature of some of their organizational missions. Thus, these organizations allow for a way to estimate the total number of adherents to the Tea Party. Earlier, I showed that while the composition of local Tea Party organizations may have changed between the first and second phases of the Tea Party, the overall numbers remained about the same: estimated to be around 1,000 before and after 2010. The real change in the organizational dimension of the Tea Party came in the number of supporters attracted to the major national organizations described in the previous section.

The data that I used for Figure 2.2 come from the IREHR. Researchers at IREHR have routinely collected information on the size of the membership of these major Tea Party organizations using surveys and other methods and graciously shared it with others. They face some of the same difficulties of counting that I described earlier in this chapter for the number of local Tea Party organizations. And to be clear, they do not count all of the people who support the idea of the Tea Party, rather the size of the membership of these specific national organizations. Since these are some of the largest, and have connections to many local affiliates, the data provide a useful way to study Tea Party organizations over time. Who counts as a member of one of these Tea Party organizations is difficult to verify, but IREHR has regularly applied the same method of counting, thus, its data can be used as a reliable estimate over time, if not a pinpoint count.

What we can see from Figure 2.2 is the shift in membership from the first to the second phase of the Tea Party movement. At the tail end of the first phase, by June 2010, there was an even distribution of membership across these six organizations (recall that Tea Party Express did not have a strategy to grow members, so the very small membership is not surprising). Of the decentralized, member-focused national organizations, PAN had the largest membership, slightly more than 70,000 strong. PAN was in existence prior to 2009 under the name, ResistNet, thus it had a jump on the others in terms of organizing and membership. The TPP were next in membership size, followed by Tea Party Nation. For TPP, they grew through building a national movement of local chapters, in a manner akin to the federated style of political movements throughout much of U.S. history. The large membership of TPP owed a lot to the local organizing and founding of hundreds of organizations in just a year. The small number of members associated with FreedomWorks is also intriguing. They began with a relatively small membership size and ranked fourth at the end of the first phase of the Tea Party.

As we move from the first to the second phase, we see great change in the membership size of these large national organizations. For four of the organizations, membership grew at a rate between 20% and 50%, between 2010 and 2013. The 1776 Tea Party experienced rapid growth, but the overall membership remained the second smallest in 2013, ahead of only TPE. The two for-profit organizations, PAN and Tea Party Nation, at the

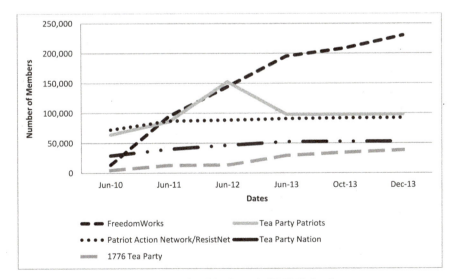

Figure 2.2 National Tea Party Membership Growth (IREHR data)

center of the Tea Party in 2010, both grew in size, but were no longer the primary membership organizations in 2013.

The most interesting and major growth was for FreedomWorks. FreedomWorks, which had one of the smallest memberships in the first phase, expanded its membership from under 14,000 to more than 200,000. FreedomWorks grew to have the largest group of members, and made up nearly half (44%) of all Tea Party members in 2013.

Examining the Tea Party across the first two phases from this perspective allows for a better understanding of the changing composition and maturation of the movement, the shift in prominence of the major national organizations, and suggests certain directions for the future. As these numbers show, there was a shift in the type of organization that most Tea Party supporters affiliated. The nationally focused FreedomWorks gained membership at a much faster rate than the more locally focused and outside tactic–oriented TPP that had been so prominent at the start of the movement. What those people were doing between the first and second phase also changed. The frequent and large protests of the first phase dwindled as we moved into the second phase. For example, Alex Seitz-Wald reported on the steep decline in attendance at Independence Day protests from 2010 to 2011.[39] Recall, April Tax Day protests across the country were a chief motivator for organizational formation in 2009. These protests continued into Tax Day 2010 where thousands of Tea Party supporters met in numerous cities. But the change from 2010 to 2011 was remarkable. Seitz-Wald reported that in Denver, 2,000 met in 2010, but just "hundreds" in 2011. In Chicago, turnout shrunk from around 1,500 in 2010 to "several hundred" just one year later. In Tulsa, thousands met in 2010, but "less than 30" came out in 2011. Overall, Seitz-Wald estimated that in 13 rallies across the country, over 25,000 turned out in 2010, but less than 4,000 in 2011.

CONCLUSION

What conclusions can we draw from the variation across Tea Party organizations and the shift from the first to the second phase of the Tea Party movement? Skocpol and Williamson showed that the Tea Party did not follow the federated style of previous U.S. political movements. This made the Tea Party quite different from earlier movements such as the women's movement or the antitax movement. Skocpol and Williamson wrote: "The Tea Party does not manifest this classic pattern of federated activity, in which local groups elect higher-level leaders."[40] But this nonfederated pattern of organizing did not occur randomly, and it was purposeful and by design. Alan McBride (quoting Zachary Courser) wrote: "Freedomworks and Tea Party Express, two umbrella national Tea Party organizations, have actively encouraged 'the disorganized nature of the movement.'"[41] And Berry et al. described the decentralized, loosely structured system as an asset to the effectiveness of the Tea Party. Decentralization meant an inside lobbying approach was not possible for much of the first phase, but protesting and fomenting public outrage could be part of an outside strategy. Berry et al. suggested, "The effectiveness of these protests taught the Tea Party that it wasn't necessary to engage in large scale mobilization to be successful but, rather, that America was in an uproar and that it didn't need to do much to catalyze a revolution to take down the Obama administration."[42]

These assessments of the Tea Party movement are all valid, particularly of the first phase of the movement. But in this book, I aim to answer the question of who was in charge with particular attention paid to the shift from the first to the second phase of the movement. The evidence so far is mixed about who has led the movement, but it appears as though the first phase was much more focused at the local level and loosely overseen by decentralized national organizations, and that in moving to the second, different national nonprofit organizations asserted more control or at least gathered more prominence. First, the research by Theda Skocpol and Vanessa Williamson showed that local organizations peaked at the end of the first phase, by November 2010, and then declined considerably a year into the second phase. Second, the evidence from IREHR showed that over the same time frame, membership in national organizations increased at a much faster rate for FreedomWorks, than for the more locally focused TPP. Third, the strategies employed by many of the national organizations shifted from mainly organizing and protesting, outside strategies, to electioneering and influencing policy. Fourth, these prominent organizations grew increasingly institutionalized and professionalized. The focus of the movement shifted to Washington and to the increasingly significant role of Tea Party members of Congress, the subject of Chapter 4 of the book.

What this suggests is that the Tea Party movement evolved or matured from the first to the second phase from a fast-moving, organizing, and protest-oriented movement to a more institutionalized, professionalized, and policy-centered movement. The first assessment of the Tea Party movement as un-federated and decentralized may characterize the early period, but the second phase may have been a bridge to a much more traditional, centralized, and federated system. If this is the direction of the Tea Party movement, it will be consistent with the style of other political movements in U.S. history, such as the antitax movement, that have typically had a strong center and steeper hierarchies. In the closing chapter of the book, I look ahead to this as a potential direction for the future of the Tea Party.[43] Until then, there are other aspects of the Tea Party to be considered, particularly who joined these various Tea Party organizations, what did they believe, and which policy issues did they care most about. Also, for whom did these Tea Party supporters vote, and what did those candidates elected as a part of the Tea Party ultimately do in Washington? The next several chapters address these questions.

Chapter 3

Tea Partiers:
The People and Their Beliefs

Writing in his local Hampton Roads, Virginia, newspaper, the *Virginia Pilot*, Cory Dillard described his commitment to the Tea Party cause and his local role:

My involvement with the tea party movement goes back to its local beginnings in 2009. . . . With the other co-founders, we planned and put on the first Tax Day Tea Party in Town Center. . . . At that point, the movement was as mad with the Republican Party as with the Democratic Party. As a true accountability movement, in our infancy, we sought to educate people about what was really going on in Washington, how a culture of corruption—in place long before the Obama ascendancy—had conspired to, on April 15 of that year, place my then-unborn daughter approximately $142,000 in debt.[1]

Dillard was drawn to the Tea Party movement for similar reasons as others across the country: disenchantment with the two national political parties, anger at the corruption of Washington, and a deep concern about the state of national finance. His attraction to the idea of the Tea Party led him to become involved in the organizational and planning activities that dominated the first phase of the movement described in Chapter 2.

But Dillard went on to write of his disappointment with the movement. He criticized the shift from focusing on the grassroots to seeking political power: "When the party chose the latter in 2010, a very ugly side of the movement emerged. . . . The tactics of the movement, however- the near-hostage holding of legislators on the national and local levels and now a complete shutdown of the federal government—show the group has diverged from what I envisioned back in early 2009." As the previous chapter documented, the move from the first to the second phase of the movement came with a shift in emphasis for organizations like Tea Party Patriots and FreedomWorks from organizing to influencing elections and policy.

Dillard ended his article by writing: "As a person who tries to put forth valid solutions to the problems of the day, I cannot continue to be aligned with a movement that would rather burn a house than work to put out its fire, whose victories history may largely record as pyrrhic." Like for others, the change in the tactics and tone of the Tea Party was too much for Dillard to handle. He could not remain committed to a movement in which he did not believe.

Cory Dillard's history with the Tea Party illustrates the importance of individuals in the movement, and the very different ways individuals, supporters, and those aligned with the ideas and organizations of the Tea Party confronted the shift from the first to the second phase. In the widespread attention given to the formation of Tea Party organizations, and jostling for position as the national voice of the movement, the grassroots members of the Tea Party have often been left out. And when they have been included in the debate, they are often described in gross generalities that overstate the homogeneity of the movement.

To that point, Dillard was also atypical of the Tea Party because of his race. Dillard is African American, and also a navy veteran, who served in the Middle East and at Guantanamo Bay. Much of the research on the people of the Tea Party movement has concluded that most were white and many racist, anti-immigrant, and mobilized by the racial antagonism associated with dog whistle politics. While this may characterize some of the supporters, the story of Cory Dillard suggests that perhaps it is a little more complicated. While many in the movement were old, white, and Republican, others were not, and they have been largely left out of the major explanations of the history of the Tea Party. There were Tea Party members who voted for Democrats, there were Libertarian Party Tea Party members who supported the legalization of marijuana, and there were women Tea Party members who approved of a strong role for government in social issues. The aim of this chapter is to delve into the supporters of the Tea Party, figure out where the diversity exists in the beliefs and attitudes of supporters, and how those may have changed from the first to the second phase of the movement.

My approach to this chapter relies on the traditions of political behavior scholars. Behaviorists, an eclectic group for sure, tend to focus on explaining why individuals behave or act related to politics in the ways they do. Behaviorists track political acts such as voting, protesting, and joining to underlying ideological values, beliefs, and political attitudes. They pay particular attention to differences in these variables across demographic groups and, increasingly, at the intersectionality of these relationships: how race, ethnicity, sex, and sexual preference interact with beliefs and actions.[2] Behaviorists frequently rely on surveys, polling, and public opinion to analyze these variables and how they change over time. In this chapter, I take advantage of the excellent data behaviorists have collected on the Tea Party.

Behaviorists focus on individuals, but most do not ignore or deny the importance of institutions. Individuals interact with a variety of political institutions. Individuals can change institutions through political acts, but individuals may also be changed by institutions. For example, Matt Grossmann coined the term "behavioral pluralism" to explain the way characteristics within social groups are reflected in the interest groups that represent them.[3] Grossmann wrote: "The strongest and most consistent factors associated with generating an extensive, prominent, and involved organized leadership are a constituency's political efficacy, its membership in local civic associations, and its voting rate."[4] These two levels of analysis, the individual and the institutional group, interact in important ways. The difference between institutionalists and behavioralists, then, is one of focus; these are not incompatible or inconsistent approaches to explaining politics.

As such, and much as Grossmann suggests, I look to understand the people of the Tea Party movement in the context of the organizations described in Chapter 2. I rely on the extant research on Tea Party supporters and members drawn from representative sample surveys and national polling data. Much of the existing research from political behaviorists aimed to explain the demographic characteristics of the average Tea Party and what the average Tea Party supporter believed. Christopher Parker and Matt Barreto's *Change They Can't Believe In* and Alan Abramowitz's "Grand Old Tea Party" represent some of the most important analyses in this vein. My aim is a little bit different in this chapter.[5] I seek out differences in the beliefs of those who support the Tea Party, drawing distinctions rather than seeking general explanations. As such, my aim here is to explain some of the major factions or camps that exist within the Tea Party, understanding that those factions may be small and make up a minority of Tea Party supporters. I begin by summarizing some of the general findings from political behaviorists on the Tea Party; then I explain several of the major divisions within the Tea Party: conservative and libertarian, Republican and Democrat; and men and women. I draw particular attention to changes in the beliefs and number of supporters of the Tea Party from the first to the second phase of the Tea Party movement.

CHANGING SUPPORT FOR THE TEA PARTY: FIRST AND SECOND PHASE

While the roots of the Tea Party may have grown prior to 2009, most polling did not commence until that year, which is widely acknowledged as the start of the first phase of the movement. Most of what we know about the people of the Tea Party, thus, begins in that year and has continued at regular intervals into the second phase ever since.

The first phase of the Tea Party was defined by high levels of favorability, particularly high given how novel the idea was for most Americans. From early polling by Gallup, we know that overall support for the movement began at around 28%, and peaked at 32% at the end of 2010.[6] This is a noteworthy level of support given public attitudes for other American institutions at the time. Confidence in Congress, for example, was under 20%, as was confidence in organized labor (20%) and big business (19%).[7] The general public barely had more confidence in the Supreme Court (36%) than the level of support for Tea Party, a movement with just a few months of life.

Opposition to the Tea Party tracked closely with support, starting at around 26% in 2009, and rising and falling in tandem with the percentage of support (see Figure 3.1). Given that during the first phase the movement had only weak connections with one of the two major political parties, a set of brand new organizations, and no coordinated communications strategy, these levels of support and opposition are remarkable. The fact that so many Americans knew what the Tea Party was is a testament to the power of the idea and the role of digital communications technologies and mass media (a subject raised in Chapter 2 and one I return to in Chapter 4).

As we move from the first to the second phase of the Tea Party movement, overall support for the Tea Party declined substantially. The percentage of Tea Party supporters dipped to as low as 21% toward the end of 2011, trended up, but then fell back down to 22% in the middle of 2014. Opposition grew steadily during this same time period. Opposition was as low as 21% in the run-up to the 2012 election, but quickly climbed to 29%, and peaked at 30% in 2014. As intriguing as the rapid increase in support noted earlier was this precipitous decline that occurred later. Recall from Chapter 2 that during the second phase, the national Tea Party organizations became more centralized, institutionalized, and formalized. Despite these advances in the organizational structure, the general public

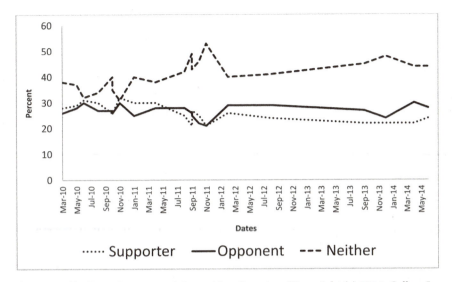

Figure 3.1 Tea Party Support and Opposition Overtime (Copyright (c) 2014, Gallup, Inc. All rights reserved. Content is used by permission; however, Gallup retains all rights of republication. Online at http://www.gallup.com/poll/147635/tea-party-movement.aspx)

reacted with decreasing levels of support, which also potentially related to the changing mass media coverage of the movement (which I return to in Chapter 4). Another notable trend from the public opinion data about the Tea Party is the steadily rising apathy toward the movement. During the first phase, mid-2010, a third (38%) of those polled considered themselves *neither* a "supporter" nor an "opponent." As the movement proceeded into the second phase, support and opposition shifted several percentage points in opposite directions, but the category of "neither" changed dramatically, driven in part by a declining number of those polled responding "no opinion." In early 2011, "neither" rose to 40%, peaked at 52% at the end of 2012, before settling down between 40% and 44% through 2014. The growing apathy or disinterest in the movement among the public coincides closely with declining participation in Tea Party organizations. The second phase is in part defined by this shift from high levels of excitement to growing disenchantment and disinterest.

As interesting as these aggregate figures are polling numbers on those likely to be supportive of the movement. The Pew Research Center tracked Republican and Republican-leaning opinion from 2009 to 2014. In the early time period, nearly half of that Republican-aligned group said that they agreed with the Tea Party, and only 3% disagreed.[8] During much of the first phase of the movement, these levels of agreement and disagreement remained steady. But as we move into the second phase, the portion of those in agreement quickly decreased and the portion in disagreement grew. By 2014, just a third of Republican and Republican-leaners reported that they agreed with the Tea Party, and 11% said they disagreed. The change seemed to come mainly from moderate or liberal Republicans. Pew compared favorability ratings between June 2013 and October 2013. During this time period, the favorability rating of moderate/liberal Republicans went from about half (46%) down to a little more than a quarter (27%). Conservative Republicans remained more supportive, but they too became less enchanted with the Tea Party, decreasing from 74% favorable to 65% favorable in less than a year.

Tea Party support and opposition among Democrats also changed. Not surprisingly, Democrats were never supportive of the Tea Party in larger numbers, but during the first phase of the Tea Party, un-favorability ratings remained relatively low. In February 2010, a third of Democrats viewed the Tea Party unfavorably, not that much more than the 15% who viewed it favorably. During the first phase, Democrats remained undecided or unsure about the Tea Party. Over time, this shifted considerably. In the second phase, favorability among Democrats dipped into the teens (17% in August of 2011 and 13% in October 2013), but the dramatic change was in un-favorability, increasing to two-thirds by August 2011 and up to 69% by October 2013. Democrats appear to have awoken more slowly to the Tea Party, and, once awake, adopted more hostile views during the second phase. In Chapter 4, I show how these changes in attitudes may relate to the increasingly prominent and critical role played by the progressive-leaning MSNBC. Thus, over this time period, Tea Party support grew rapidly during the first phase, but then later fell back down in the second phase.

As support in the Tea Party waned overall, there were also changes in the demographics of support. In 2013 alone, according to the Pew Research Center, support among whites declined from 42% in June to 31% in October. Similar declines occurred for most other demographic categories with the exception of Hispanic Americans who increased favorability from 25% to 30%. Thus as the Tea Party movement moved from the first to the second phase, support declined overall, but also within those groups, whites, males, and older citizens, who were most enthusiastic early on.[9]

The patterns of support for the Tea Party track closely with what we saw in Chapter 2 for the organizations of the Tea Party. Support and organizational formation grew quickly and spiked during the first phase. Support weakened at the same time organizations stopped forming, and some closed, during the second phase of the movement.

GENERAL ATTITUDES AND DEMOGRAPHICS OF
TEA PARTY SUPPORTERS

As important as the changing levels of support for the idea of the Tea Party is what Tea Party supporters actually believed. We know the most about the general political attitudes of those in the Tea Party from the research of Christopher Parker and Matt Barreto, published in *Change They Can't Believe In: The Tea Party and Reactionary Politics in America.*[10] Their research was based on an original stratified sample survey in seven states (Georgia, Michigan, Missouri, Nevada, North Carolina, Ohio, and California) conducted in 2010 and then again in 2011. They compared "true believers" in the Tea Party with "true skeptics" and found consistently different demographics and attitudes. True believers were more likely to be white (84% compared to 60% of true skeptics); male (59% versus 47% of true skeptics); and Born Again Christians (52% compared to 30% of true skeptics). True believers in the Tea Party were also less likely to be younger (11% were between 18 and 29 compared to 18% of true skeptics) and relatively poor (11% made less than $20,000 a year compared to 18% of true skeptics). Using similar methods, Alan Abramowitz also showed that Tea Party supporters were more likely to be white, male, and older than nonsupporters. Compared to nonsupporters, a majority of Tea Party supporters were over the age of 45 (70% versus 59%), white (85% versus 75%), and male (63% versus 45%).[11]

On the issues, Abramowitz also showed the great differences between the beliefs of Tea Party supporters and nonsupporters.[12] On policy issues, supporters of the Tea Party were more likely to oppose health care reform (81%), oppose the economic stimulus plan (87%), and oppose policies that promoted clean energy (74%) than nonsupporters. These large majorities suggest a level of consensus across Tea Party supporters on certain key policy issues. The beliefs about these issues also track closely with antipathy for President Obama as well as for his fellow Democrats, Senate Majority Leader Harry Reid (NV) and Congresswoman Nancy Pelosi (CA). According to Pew, nearly all Tea Party supporters had an unfavorable view of Pelosi (93%) and also of Reid (82%). But it was President Obama who ran for office on a platform connected to health care and clean energy, who was later compelled to incorporate economic stimulus into his initial policy agenda because of the economic downturn at the end of 2008, who drew the most ire from the Tea Party. Ninety-six percent of Tea Party supporters had an unfavorable view of the president and 77% had a *very* unfavorable view. The very same issues that the president championed in the early days of his presidency were the issues that many Tea Party supporters condemned so loudly.

This relationship between President Obama and the Tea Party cannot be overstated. The president played a significant role in seemingly every attitude of those in the movement, and the importance of the president's race cannot be ignored.[13] In fact, some of the most notable and damning findings on the Tea Party relate to issues of race, ethnicity, and sexual preference. Parker and Barreto revealed the ideologies and aspects of racial attitudes of Tea Party supporters.[14] True believers in the Tea Party were much more likely to have "Fear of Obama" (67% compared to 7% of true skeptics) and were labeled by the researchers as holding racist views (42% compared to 14% of true skeptics). True believers were much more likely to support racial profiling and indefinite detainment of suspected terrorists, and less likely to support the Development, Relief, and Education for Alien Minors (DREAM) Act.[15] Based on their analysis, Parker and Barreto concluded that "the data suggests that supporters of the Tea Party are statistically more likely to hold negative attitudes toward immigrants and sexual minorities across a range of different issues and topics, and are firmly opposed to the idea of group equality."[16]

It seems true that most Tea Party supporters took a different stance on immigration than the public in general, but the extent of that difference may have softened over time. Polling by the Pew Research Center in early 2014 showed that three-quarters of the public agreed that there should be a path to citizenship "if they meet certain requirements," while for Republicans the figure is around two-thirds (66%). What is most interesting is that the figure for Tea Party Republicans is less, but still 59% agreed, a majority of that group.[17] This finding may relate to the later time period of the polling, conducted several years after the major work by Parker and Barreto and also during the second phase of the Tea Party. But Parker and Barreto also noted the importance of the intensity of the sentiments about immigration. For example, 52% of Tea Party supporters who regularly vote—arguably the most engaged supporters of the movement—supported a path to citizenship, and 37% of those engaged Tea Party supporters believed that there should be a "national effort to deport" those in the country without documentation (compared to 17% of those polled overall). This suggests that one of the differences that exist within the Tea Party is between those most energized and active and those who only passively support the movement. The strength of political attitudes held by those in the Tea Party closely tracks with the strength of the pull toward the movement.

The general pattern of Tea Party support has been in white, male, and relatively wealthy demographics. Research further suggests that the Tea Party ideology is sharply pro-liberty, anti-minority, and anti-equality. And on policy issues, Tea Party supporters generally opposed President Obama on health care, fiscal issues, and immigration reform. Again, these are findings that aimed to explain the general patterns of the Tea Party. In the next several sections, I attempt to draw distinctions within the Tea Party. I seek out areas of heterogeneity across important factions of the Tea Party.

GEOGRAPHIC DIVISIONS OF TEA PARTY SUPPORTERS

Based in part on the general findings discussed earlier, early impressions of the Tea Party were that it was a regional movement: occurring mainly in the South. Political historians tracked the dominant Tea Party ideology to southern antecedents in antitax, pro-segregation, and antiforeigner movements of the past.[18] Illustrative of this, the national organization, the Tea Party Patriots, was founded in Georgia and many of the early Tea Party rallies occurred in southern cities.

But the best numbers available show that, while there were more members in southern states, the other three regions of the country had substantial numbers of Tea Party supporters. Remember from the previous chapter that these membership totals represent individuals who were affiliated with one of the national organizations, thus not a count of the total number of individuals who support the ideals of the Tea Party.[19] However, it seems reasonable to assume there is a strong positive correlation between these two different variables such that the numbers provided in the figure represent a reasonable approximation of the larger trend of support.

In 2010, at the tail end of the first phase of the Tea Party movement, around 42% of supporters were in the South, 23% in the West, 19% in the Midwest, and 15% in the Northeast. Contrary to common expectations, this suggests a broader national movement with more prominence in the southern states but interest in all parts of the country. And other social science research corroborates these findings. Based on 2010 polling data, McBride found that controlling for other factors such as party affiliation and conservatism, "southerners are only marginally more likely to be supportive (of the Tea Party) than non-southerners."[20]

A number of years on, the second phase of the Tea Party saw only a small shift in where Tea Party members lived. There were increases in Tea Party support in the South, somewhat greater than in other parts of the country. Between 2011 and 2012, Tea Party members in the South grew 30%, versus 26% in the Midwest, 24% in the West, and merely 18% in the Northeast. Though the pace of change differed, the regional breakdown of Tea Party supporters remained similar in the second phase of the movement.

Tea Party members were spread out across the country, but Tea Party views also seem to differ by region. Scholars have long showed that there

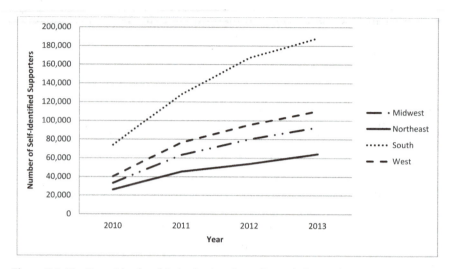

Figure 3.2 Tea Party Membership by Region (http://www.irehr.org/issue-areas/tea-party-nationalism/tea-party-news-and-analysis/item/527-status-of-tea-party-by-the-numbers)

are great regional and state differences in the United States. Political pundits contend that states are either "red" or "blue" depending on whether a majority in the state supports the Republican or the Democratic candidate for the presidency. Others have looked further back to explain patterns of differences across states. Daniel Elazar famously explained that state political culture differs from state to state based on differences in historic immigration and religious patterns.[21] According to Elazar, state political culture is traditionalistic, individualistic, or moralistic. And Erickson et al. later contended that public opinion drives state political ideology in more liberal or conservative directions.[22] They argued that state legislators respond as much to their party as to these variations in public opinion when they design and change policy. Thus, there are a number of ways that scholars have used to link the views of individuals to patterns across states.

Some of these differences seem to show up when we look at the people of the Tea Party. Alan McBride examined polling data from 2010 and compared Tea Party supporters in the South with those living outside of the South.[23] McBride found those in the South tended to have a more disapproving view of President Obama, particularly as it related to how he handled the economy and imposed new regulations on businesses. On social issues, though, McBride showed similarity on the issue of abortion. Around 60% of southern and non-southern Tea Party supporters favored overturning the 1973 Supreme Court decision, *Roe v. Wade*. But differences appear when McBride looked at ideology and partisanship. Just a third (36%) of Tea Party adherents in the East self-identified as conservative and a third (36%) of them as Republicans. A similar percentage (39%) of those living in western states identified as conservative. The real difference shows up when McBride compared this to Tea Party members living in other parts of the country. A majority (52%) of Tea Party members in the South and 47% in the Midwest identify as conservative. The Tea Party movement may have nominally been a national movement, but who was drawn in each region differed greatly: conservatives in the South and Midwest and nonconservatives in the East and West. These regional distinctions are important to take note of when seeking to understand the Tea Party, particularly the legislative behavior of Tea Party members of Congress elected in different states.

Other research supports these findings. Stacy Ulbig and Sarah Macha showed that Tea Party supporters in the West were drawn to the movement primarily based on anti-immigration views.[24] Many of these individuals lived in states along the Mexico border, such as Arizona and New Mexico, where immigration policy has been hotly contested since the early 2000s. Individuals in these states have been organizing groups, such as the Minutemen, to patrol the border and have been lobbying for legislation, such as Arizona 1070, to tighten state immigration enforcement.[25] And the leaders of anti-immigration organizations have also been active in certain Tea Party organizations and at Tea Party events in the West. The Institute for Research and Education on Human Rights (IREHR) found over a hundred such relationships. For example, Bob Wright was the state director of the Minuteman Civil Defense Corps—New Mexico chapter and also spoke at a New Mexico Tea Party event. Jeff Schwilk was a team leader of the San Diego (CA) Minutemen and a leader of Social Patriots, and Pat Byrne was Texas state deputy director of the Minutemen Civil Defense Corps (TX Chapter) and executive director of Patriots Coalition.[26] This political environment that has been so influenced by border politics is somewhat unique to western states and seems to overlap with the political priorities of Tea Party supporters in those states.

Conversely, Tea Party supporters in the East, where immigration issues were much less salient, were drawn to the movement mainly because of economic issues. During the first phase of the Tea Party, unemployment hit new highs across the country, and certain states in the Northeast, particularly New York and Delaware, were hit hardest by job losses. Recall the findings from the previous chapter that the location of Tea Party rallies correlated strongly with the number of foreclosures, suggesting that economic factors mattered both to the organizational and attitudinal dimensions of the movement.

Tea Party supporters in the Midwest were attracted because of a strong antigovernment belief (the chance of being a Tea Party supporter in the Midwest increases from 3% to 18% for those who believe government "is more a part of the problem than the solution"). In the South, where the largest number of Tea Party supporters resided, there was a mix of economic and antigovernment beliefs that drew supporters.

These regional and geographic differences suggest that Tea Party supporters were not drawn to the movement for the exact same reasons. The idea of a Tea Party likely sparked disenchantment with the local or state political status quo, but since states differ so greatly, what Tea Party supporters in each region believed was quite different. This finding of regional differences contributed to Stacy Ulbig and Sarah Macha concluding: "Counter to much popular sentiment, we find that racism plays no role in predicting movement support, either. Though Tea Party supporters are more likely to be white Southerners and to express more racist attitudes, these attitudes do not appear to cause a person to support the movement."[27] Notwithstanding this statistical conclusion, even if racism and Tea Party support were not causally related, the connection between certain negative attitudes toward racially significant policies and support for the Tea Party poses serious concerns for the identity of the Tea Party movement and should worry many interested in American politics. Racist attitudes may not have caused Tea Party support, but too often these views dominated the imagery, rhetoric, and agenda of the movement, as they have for decades in other elements of politics based in the South. I return to this theme in the conclusion of the book.

DIVISIONS OF THE REPUBLICAN PARTY: TEA PARTY REPUBLICANS AND NON–TEA PARTY REPUBLICANS

Since we know that Tea Party members have been somewhat, though not exclusively, clustered in southern states, many have concluded that they also must cluster in purely partisan ways as well, since many southern states have trended toward the GOP and many were solidly red states during recent presidential elections. If so, then those affiliated with the Tea Party and the Republican Party should hold similar ideological views on policy.

This argument is largely the one made by Hans Noel in *Political Ideologies and Political Parties in America*. His general argument was that recent political polarization in the United States is the result of dominant ideologies elbowing into the midsection of the two major political parties. About the Tea Party, he wrote: "The [Tea Party] movement represents adherents of an ideology, who wish for that ideology to be adopted by a political party.... What is more, they have been successful. Their ideology has been largely adopted by the Republicans."[28]

In general, this thesis is correct and substantiated by evidence. But on a number of important issues, according to research by Ronald Rapoport et al., the situation is a little more complicated. For example, on environmental regulations, affirmative action, and education policy, there were large differences for Republicans. Tea Party-affiliated Republicans opposed environmental regulations much more so than non-Tea Party Republicans (86% versus 19%). A much larger percentage of Tea Party Republicans also opposed affirmative action (86% versus 19%) and supported the closing of the Department of Education (76% versus 10%).[29]

These differences also related to the ranking of policy priorities. A larger portion of Tea Party Republicans believed that abortion, shrinking government, and repealing the Affordability Care Act (the name of health care law or Obamacare) were "top priorities" compared to non-Tea Party Republicans. Conversely, a larger portion of non-Tea Party Republicans placed deficit reduction, jobs, and immigration as a "top priority" compared to Tea Party Republicans.

But individuals approach politics with different levels of enthusiasm: most Americans are largely passive participants in politics; a scant few are active on a daily basis. Rapoport et al. showed striking similarities between Tea Party supporters and Tea Party activists. These researchers compared survey respondents who were members of FreedomWorks, the national Tea Party organization described in the previous chapter (what they label as "Tea Party activists") to respondents who supported the Tea Party, but were not FreedomWorks members (what they label as "Tea Party supporters"). They found that activists were only slightly more conservative on issues, around five percentage points more on most issues. For example, 91% of Tea Party activists opposed environmental regulations compared to 86% of nonactivist Tea Party supporters, a relatively minor difference. For the Tea Party, the level of enthusiasm and engagement does not relate strongly to different policy attitudes.

The real differences appear between Republicans who were and were not tied to the Tea Party. The authors of that research concluded that "the divide between the two groups of Republicans (Tea Party and non-Tea Party) is so wide that on four of eleven issues, the non-Tea Party Republicans are actually closer to the mean of the Democratic identifiers in the sample than they were to the Tea party Republicans."[30] This is a rather shocking finding since it suggests just how far Tea Party Republicans are from the views of the majority of Americans who are Democrats, Independents, or non-Tea Party Republicans. These findings also suggest a level of disunity and disagreement within the Republican Party. These differences within the GOP portended the intraparty squabbles to support candidates for elected office in 2010 and 2012, and then the combative legislative behavior of Tea Party Republican members of Congress that I detail in Chapters 4 and 5. As Noel contended, the Republican Party has largely responded to the Tea Party wing of the party and grown ever more distant from the beliefs and attitudes of non-Tea Party Republicans.[31]

One parallel to these differences between Tea Party Republicans and non–Tea Party Republicans may be related to how each group consumes political media. This is a particularly important consideration for a new political phenomenon like the Tea Party. Unlike beliefs about previous movements for civil rights or women's rights, the contemporary Tea Party was not yet a part of the school curriculum in 2009, thus most Americans learned about what the Tea Party meant as it was happening, either through personal conversations or by attending organizational meetings, but most likely through the mass media. Jacobson found that Tea Party Republicans were the most likely to turn to Fox News (Sean Hannity and Mike Hucka-bee, in particular) on television and conservative radio (including Rush Limbaugh, Glenn Beck, and Mark Levin).[32] Nearly three-quarters (71%) of the audience of conservative media were Tea Party supporters. Non–Tea Party Republicans also turn to conservative media, but to a much lesser extent. The intensity of mass media usage also differed in important ways. Over a third of Tea Party Republicans used four or more conservative sources for news compared to just 5.8% of non-Tea Party Republicans. Tea Party Republicans were not just passively learning about the Tea Party; they were intently tuned to particular news outlets, often to the exclusion of other sources of information. Nearly half (44.5%) of Tea Party Republicans report using no mainstream sources of news, compared to 3.7% of non-Tea Party Republicans (and 30% of Democrats). To be clear, it is not evident whether it is the substance of the news coverage that drives viewers to support or oppose the Tea Party. There is no evidence that those undecided about the Tea Party have been swayed by exclusively listening to Glenn Beck. Those who listen to Glenn Beck were likely latent Tea Party supporters or existing supporters seeking more information. Rather, the correlation between the source of news and the opinions of viewers may show that there is a feedback loop between a self-selected population of Tea Party viewers that reinforces their existing views, but even that effect may be tenuous. We know from research by Arceneaux and Johnson that the polarization of cable news broadcasts may merely sort viewers by pre-existing ideology, but not significantly shift or strengthen views.[33] We can safely conclude from extant research that Tea Party Republicans have different mass media consumption habits from other Republicans and also

Democrats, and that these differences are demonstrated in what they consume and how much of it they consume. The evidence is not clear, though, the extent to which consuming a lot of conservative news changed the views of Tea Party supporters.

So far, we know that variation exists within the dominant Republican-affiliated wing of the Tea Party movement, but the research by Rapoport et al. also showed other differences. Many non-Republican Tea Party supporters were Independents or unaffiliated with a political party, but there were also small, but significant, numbers of Tea Party Democrats. Estimates range from as low as 4% to as high as 15% of all Tea Party supporters who claimed to be affiliated with the Democratic Party.[34] Polling done by Gallup in April 2014 showed that Democrats (conservative, moderate, and liberal) made up 24% of the supporters of the Tea Party. This is a truly surprising finding for most casual observers of the movement. The reality of a Tea Party Democrat, according to most of the commentary on the Tea Party, sounds something like a unicorn or a four-leaf clover. But this polling evidence suggests that Tea Party Democrats do in fact exist and that they are far from a rarity. Illustrative of this, Gary Boisclair ran unsuccessfully to unseat Congressman Keith Ellison in the Democratic primary in Minnesota. Boisclair ran as a pro-life Democrat and aired fiercely antiabortion advertisements in the campaign. He was also, according to his biography, a "Tea Party Activist." Ellison easily won the contest, but it should not be ignored that Boisclair self-identified as a Tea Party activist and a Democrat. While Tea Party Democrats are a small minority of the movement, it is still important to acknowledge their existence, and to continue to study how they fit into this movement. The existence of Tea Party Democrats also suggests potential directions for the future of the Tea Party that I return to in Chapter 6.

DIVISIONS OF THE TEA PARTY: CONSERVATIVES AND NONCONSERVATIVES

General findings, like those presented earlier, lead some to conclude that many Tea Party members, particularly those not affiliated with the Democratic Party, were simply the most conservative Republican Party members. They reason that with just two major parties in the United States, each party acts as a "big tent" under which individuals fall somewhere along a continuum of beliefs. On occasion, such as during the 1960s within the Democratic Party, particular wings of the party got energized by newly salient issues: the Vietnam War for the liberal wing of the Democratic Party in 1968, and the Great Recession and the election of Barack Obama in

2009. The Tea Party may just be the name given to this conservative wing of the Republican Party that has pushed the party to a more ideologically pure position.[35]

And in 2011 no less than Robert Putnam—one of the titans of studying American political behavior most famously associated with the book and the phrase *Bowling Alone*—weighed in on this feature of the Tea Party! Writing in the *New York Times*, Putnam and his coauthor, David Campbell, wrote: "Actually, the Tea Party's supporters today were highly partisan Republicans long before the Tea Party was born, and were more likely than others to have contacted government officials. In fact, past Republican affiliation is the single strongest predictor of Tea Party support today."[36] They based their conclusions on interviews with a representative sample of 3,000 citizens starting in 2006. The timing of their research permitted them to track Tea Party supporters to before 2009, the formal starting point for the movement. They continued: "What's more, contrary to some accounts, the Tea Party is not a creature of the Great Recession. Many Americans have suffered in the last four years, but they are no more likely than anyone else to support the Tea Party. And while the public image of the Tea Party focuses on a desire to shrink government, concern over big government is hardly the only or even the most important predictor of Tea Party support among voters."

Putnam and Campbell ultimately pointed to race and religion to explain the commonalities across the Tea Party. They wrote: "So what do Tea Partiers have in common? They are overwhelmingly white, but even compared to other white Republicans, they had a low regard for immigrants and blacks long before Barack Obama was president, and they still do." And they tied the Tea Party to religion and social conservatism. They concluded: "[Tea Party supporters] were disproportionately social conservatives in 2006—opposing abortion, for example—and still are today. Next to being a Republican, the strongest predictor of being a Tea Party supporter today was a desire, back in 2006, to see religion play a prominent role in politics."[37]

The Putnam and Campbell findings, based on social science methods and also tied to one of the field's celebrities, reinforced what many pundits and political commentators already believed. Joan Walsh of the online news magazine, *Salon*, for example, wrote: "It's great to have data, but this is something a lot of us believed all along—The Tea Party was the Republican base dressed up in silly costumes."[38] Or Peter Beinert, writing in the *Daily Beast* (online) about the Putnam and Campbell research, argued that "the Tea Party, in other words, isn't the alternative to the GOP's moderate, business wing. It's the successor."[39]

But much like the findings on region and differences within the Republican Party, these generalizations are sound, but not complete. Other researchers used 2010 data from the Cooperative Congressional Election Study (CCES), a web-based survey, to investigate just these partisan claims. The published results by Kevin Arceneaux and Stephen P. Nicholson showed interesting differences, particularly related to attitudes toward race.[40] They concluded: "Although we find some evidence that racial resentment colors the majority of Tea Party supporters' definition of who is deserving of government aid, it does not appear to be the driving force behind opposition to social programs. We also uncover some evidence of heterogeneity within the movement, with a small minority of Tea Party supporters voicing less extreme political attitudes and evincing a rejection of negative racial stereotypes."[41]

One of the ways that Arceneaux and Nicholson reached these unconventional and striking conclusions about the Tea Party was by comparing conservative and nonconservative Tea Party supporters, a small but real segment of supporters. They stated: "Yet a familiar pattern emerges from the data: while Tea Party supporters who do not identify as conservative take more conservative positions than everyone else, these individuals also take less-extreme and somewhat more moderate positions on racial issues."[42] For example, nonconservative Tea Party supporters were less religious and less likely to be Born Again Christians. A fifth (22%) of nonconservative Tea Party supporters were Born Again Christian (almost identical to the overall population) compared to nearly half (47%) of conservative Tea Party supporters. What explained so much about the beliefs of Tea Party members for Putnam and Campbell washes away when you pull religion out of the demographic equation. Illustrative of this, on issues, nonconservative Tea Party members had distinct views from both conservative Tea Party supporters and nonconservatives, in general. More than four-fifths (81%) of conservative Tea Party supporters strongly opposed affirmative action policies compared to fewer than a fifth (19.72%) of nonconservatives who strongly opposed affirmative action policies. Nonconservative Tea Party supporters fell somewhere in-between: two-thirds (68.63%) strongly opposed affirmative action, substantially less than conservative Tea Party supporters and much more than conservatives (36.22%), in general. The researchers found similar differences for attitudes toward immigration laws.

In looking to explain these conclusions, Arceneaux and Nicholson argued that "the differences between non-conservative and conservative Tea Party supporters do not appear to be an artifact of minorities identifying as non-conservative Tea Party supporters. Both factions of

Tea Party supporters are overwhelmingly white."[43] Nonconservative Tea Party supporters seem to be a distinct ideological cohort, distinct from conservative Tea Party supporters and nonconservatives who do not support the Tea Party. Looking ahead to the future, better understanding these Tea Party supporters would deepen our common understanding of the movement.

Parker and Barreto reached similar conclusions when they compared Tea Party conservatives and Tea Party nonconservatives. They found that Tea Party conservatives are much more likely to support civil liberties, even when they are juxtaposed with issues of terrorism, especially on issues of protecting free speech and opposing racial profiling. But these differences flip when it comes to civil rights. Non-Tea Party conservatives were more likely to support gay marriage (37% compared to 25% of Tea Party conservatives) and somewhat more likely to support gays serving openly in the military (39% compared to 34% of Tea Party conservatives). Non-Tea Party conservatives were also more likely to support the DREAM Act (50%) compared to Tea Party conservatives (30%). Even more stark distinctions appeared when the researchers compared the two groups on attitudes toward President Obama. Nearly two-thirds of non-Tea Party conservatives approved of Obama "as a person" compared to less than a third (29%) of Tea Party conservatives. Three-quarters of Tea Party conservatives (78%) hoped the president would fail compared to 36% of non-Tea Party conservatives, and just a quarter of Tea Party conservatives (25%) believed that the president was a Christian compared to 42% of non-Tea Party conservatives. Neither group held particularly high views of the president, but the degree of distrust and animosity among Tea Party conservatives divides them from other conservatives.

On the whole, the research seems to show that a large portion of the Tea Party is made up of conservative Republicans, and they hold some of the strongest conservative views on economic and social issues. These members of the Tea Party are likely to be evangelical or devout Christians, and their views are greatly informed by this level of religiosity, and also by their deep and not-so-Christian hatred of President Obama. But nonconservative Tea Party members also exist, and they hold distinct and much more centrist views on many issues. While non–Tea Party conservatives are hardly fans of President Obama, at least a majority value him as a person, and some even trust him when he explained his religious practices. This division within the conservative wing of the Tea Party movement must be understood to fully appreciate the movement in the future.

DIVISIONS OF THE TEA PARTY: TEA PARTY LIBERTARIANS AND
TEA PARTY REPUBLICANS

The excellent research on the attitudes and partisan leanings of Tea Party members supports the broad argument that many are conservative and Republican, but the differences noted by Arceneaux and Nicholson as well as by Parker and Barreto point to the other ideological side of the movement. If we look at differences on social issues and certain spending issues, the libertarian instincts of some Tea Party members that run counter to the typical conservative Republican agenda emerge. For example, a third of nonconservative Tea Party supporters believed that abortion should always be permitted, compared to just 13% of conservative Tea Party supporters. Another issue that drives the Tea Party Republicans apart is sexual rights. Fewer than half (41%) of nonconservative Tea Party supporters agreed with state bans on gay marriage compared to nearly three-quarters (72%) of conservative Tea Party supporters. Finally, while not as large in magnitude, a fifth (19%) of nonconservative Tea Party supporters condoned cuts in defense spending compared to less than a tenth (9%) of conservative Tea Party supporters.

These distinctions have not been lost on leaders at the Cato Institute, the center of libertarian thought in Washington. I return to the importance of Cato in the development of the Tea Party in Chapter 4, but the organization has publicized research about the empirical record on Tea Party views. David Kirby and Emily McClintock Ekins wrote: "Many still mistake the tea party as one large group, sharing common interests, which our research shows is incorrect. Understanding the tea party's two halves—libertarian and conservative—may help unravel the seemingly contradictory impulses of the group: If it is an independent movement, then why do tea party supporters plan to vote overwhelmingly Republican?" They continued: "On the issues, tea party libertarians are less concerned than conservatives about the moral direction of the country, gay marriage, immigration, job outsourcing and abortion."[44] But, they argued, "Libertarians, including young people who supported Ron Paul's 2008 presidential campaign, provided much of the early energy for the tea party and spread the word through social media." Cato reported on data drawn from polling by Gallup that showed Tea Party libertarians are very likely to be male (62% versus 55% of Tea Party conservatives), more likely to reside in a city (40% urban compared to just 22% of Tea Party conservatives), and less likely to attend church (29% attend "every week" compared to 48% of Tea Party conservatives). Almost by definition, Tea Party libertarians have a very different view about the appropriate role of government. Nearly two-thirds of Tea Party libertarians (63%) believed government "should have 'little' or 'no' responsibility" for "upholding 'moral standards' among its citizens" compared to just a third (37%) of Tea Party conservatives.[45] These differences led to differences in certain social policy preferences. According to polling by CBS News/*New York Times*, nearly all Tea Party libertarians (91%) were "more concerned about taxes, jobs than abortion, gay marriage" compared to two-third (67%) of Tea Party conservatives. And, according to a *Washington Post* survey, nearly all (87%) were critical of government because they believe Congress did not "cut spending" versus just 64% of Tea Party conservatives.

The Libertarian Party has much weaker organizational roots across the country compared to the Democratic and Republican parties. Affiliating with libertarian ideas remains more of an ideology for most voters, because few ever have a Libertarian Party candidate on the ballot for whom to vote. Yet, the failure to turn libertarian beliefs into an institutionalized political party does not diminish its importance in the Tea Party movement. The ideas of liberty and freedom are so important to many adherents of the Tea Party movement, but at the same time are fluid concepts important to those outside the movement. As the research shows, Democrats and Republicans both believe in liberty, and they often just disagree on which issues it is most important. Similarly, within the Tea Party supporters, those who most closely align with the values of libertarianism show great differences with other supporters. Figures, such as Ron Paul and his son Rand, Republican Party members yet so closely aligned with libertarianism, have thus featured heavily in rallying support to the movement. As such, I return to the importance of Senator Rand Paul and the growing importance of the libertarian agenda for the future of the Tea Party in Chapter 6 of the book.

DIVISIONS OF THE TEA PARTY: WOMEN AND MEN

Understanding that there are several camps within the Tea Party— conservative, libertarian, Republican, independent, and even Democrat— begs the question of who makes up these camps. Who are these Tea Party conservatives and who are the Tea Party libertarians? Researchers suggested that one answer to that question can be found in differences between men and women. While men make up the largest percentage of the Tea Party, several Tea Party leaders were women, including Sarah Palin and Michelle Bachman, and many of the founders of key Tea Party organizations were also women. Women have played a part in the Tea Party, and their opinions seem to differ from those of Tea Party men.

Melissa Deckman examined public opinion data on women and the Tea Party to see how gender might relate to movement.[46] Deckman analyzed data from a major study conducted by Pew in 2010. She showed that women affiliated with the Tea Party were more likely to be white, older, educated, and well-off financially. For example, in 2010, more than four-fifths (82.3%) of Tea Party women were white, compared to two-thirds (68.9%) of women nationally. More than a quarter (27.8%) of Tea Party women were over the age of 65 and a quarter (25.5%) had income greater than $75,000 a year. This compares to less than a fifth (18.4%) of women nationally who were over 65 years old and just a sixth (15.2%) who had income greater than $75,000.

Tea Party women are demographically distinct from women in general, but they also participate in politics differently. Tea Party women are more politically engaged than women in general: nearly all those Tea Party women polled (97.2%) were likely voters compared to 80.1% of women nationally. This is a testament to the mobilizing and energizing effect of affiliating with a social movement like the Tea Party.

On prioritizing certain issues, Tea Party women were quite similar to women in general. The same percentage of both groups believed health care, energy, economy, and terrorism were "very important" issues, but on other issues, the importance differs for Tea Party women. A larger percentage of Tea Party women thought that the federal budget, abortion, the Afghanistan war, and gay marriage were very important, while women in general prioritized the environment and the financial system to a greater extent.

For the purpose of this book, the differences between Tea Party men and women are even more compelling. Tea Party women and Tea Party men seemed to hold different ideological views on policy and prioritize issues differently. Again according to analysis by Deckman, most Tea Party women (71.2%) described themselves as either very conservative or conservative, and 80% as Republican.[47] Tea Party women were more religious (83.8% said religion is very important versus 55.4% of men), and believed social issues like gay marriage, abortion, and government support for the poor were more important, while Tea Party men were more likely to believe taxes and financial regulations to be very important. Tea Party men appeared more libertarian-oriented in their ideological outlook, and Tea Party women more conservative ideologically and Republican Party affiliated.

Thus, the evidence suggests that if we do not pay attention to gender, we will miss out on a key distinction within Tea Party supporters. These differences suggest that Tea Party men and women may be drawn to the movement for different reasons. While they each may gather under the same mantle, join similar organizations, and even live under the same roof, what they believe is often distinct. These distinctions, given that they are likely to be spread throughout the country, make it difficult for leaders of the Tea Party to gather agreement on the direction of policy and to prioritize a legislative agenda. In the next chapter, I return to the difficulty of leading the Tea Party given the variety of beliefs of adherents.

TEA PARTY AND FOREIGN POLICY VIEWS

Thus far in this chapter, I've focused mainly on explaining the behavioral differences between Tea Party supporters. Many of the key issues of the Tea Party have been U.S. domestic issues such as the budget, taxes, and regulations. These are issues that many Tea Party Republicans and Tea Party Libertarians likely agree: smaller and weaker. Foreign policy, on the other hand, is one policy area that conservatives and libertarians have historically differed, and thus an area to consider for the Tea Party.

For example, Lee Mardsen wrote: "The Tea Party itself represents a coalition of conservative evangelicals, the religious right, and libertarians united at the domestic level by the demand for smaller government and lower taxes but *divided* on foreign policy" (emphasis added).[48] Using survey data, Brian Rathbun found that many Tea Party supporters had mainstream conservative views toward foreign affairs, rather than the strict isolationism that one might assume of those with ties to libertarianism.[49]

Polling from the Center for the People and the Press supports this claim.[50] Tea Party Republicans were more likely to support a strong military (60% compared to 38% of non-Tea Party Republicans and 20% of Democrats) and were less likely to support diplomacy (26% compared to 50% of non-Tea Party Republicans and 72% of Democrats). Tea Party Republicans also generally supported maintaining (60%) or increasing military spending (21%), even in the context of reducing the national debt, another Tea Party priority. Tea Party Republicans were less likely to support military cuts than others.[51] Tea Party Republicans also were more likely to side with Israel (79% compared to 53% of non-Tea Party Republicans and 41% of Democrats) and oppose President Obama's stance on the Israel-Palestine conflict: 68% believed that the president "favors Palestinians too much."

While foreign policy issues have not been as prominent among the Tea Party compared to other domestic and fiscal issues, foreign policy does provide an additional window into the movement and its supporters. These are particularly important to consider for the future of the movement, and also for the shift from the first to the second phase, because as

Tea Party candidates became Tea Party elected officials, they had to cast votes on foreign policy issues, not just taxing and spending issues. Chapter 5 shows just how certain foreign policy issues, including trade issues, divided Tea Party members of Congress. These divisions among Tea Party leaders reflect many of the disagreements among Tea Party supporters.

CONCLUSION

As the previous chapters have shown, from a certain perspective, the Tea Party was brand new in 2009. The novelty and excitement of this political movement, the fluidity of its core idea, and its evocative symbols drew supporters rapidly. Awareness and support for the Tea Party grew quickly and spiked during the first phase of the movement.

But the growing support for the Tea Party was not drawn from a homogeneous group of Americans. This is in part because of the nature of the Tea Party image, which was flexible and amorphous enough to mean different things for different people. Also, as I show in the next chapter, the ideas of the Tea Party pre-dated most of the organizing in 2009, having been formulated in think tanks and research institutes since the 1950s, and later promulgated by various candidates for office and political pundits. Thus, those who became supporters of the Tea Party had preexisting values and beliefs about liberty and the proper role of government that drew them to the movement. But the ambiguousness of how the Tea Party was defined by various organizations meant that different people were drawn for different reasons. Libertarians, frustrated socially conservative Republicans, Independents without a partisan home, and even some Democrats saw the idea of the Tea Party as appealing and consistent with their political views. Supporters were not drawn randomly or equally from each of these preexisting points of view. Supporters were more likely to be male, older, and registered Republicans. Supporters were also concentrated in the South. For these reasons, the dominant views of Tea Party supporters tracked with views of older, male, southern Republicans.

But the Tea Party provided a flexible vehicle for others. Tea Party libertarians with little interest in social issues came to the movement. They sought a politics of limited government, lower taxes, and fewer government incursions in private life, views that only sometimes aligned with their conservative Tea Party compatriots. Tea Party Democrats even saw the glimmer of their views reflected in the appeals to liberty that they may have felt were lacking from those in their party. And even along gender lines, Tea Party women saw a movement that could advance a very different agenda than Tea Party men.

These patterns suggest that common explanations of the beliefs of Tea Party supporters must be tempered by the empirical reality. Some in the Tea Party held deeply intolerant views toward other social groups, including African Americans, immigrants, and those in the lesbian, gay, bisexual, and transgender (LGBT) community. But these views were not universal. Others in the Tea Party had little interest in changing social policy, instead—perhaps naively—they saw the Tea Party as a way to pursue solely economic aims connected to jobs and the size of government.

However, these views that remained the abstract notion of supporters during the first phase of the Tea Party movement took on new importance in the second phase. As Tea Party candidates became Tea Party members of Congress, elected officials had to represent Tea Party constituents. If there was just one Tea Party viewpoint, the job of legislating would have been easier. Instead, new members of Congress had to decipher the complex and often inconsistent views of those inside and outside the Tea Party. While many supporters hewed in to the platform of the Republican Party, which aspects of that platform were most pressing differed greatly.

But the job of newly elected members of Congress was also complicated by other sources of support. Not every supporter of the Tea Party was an individual voter. Financial patrons provided millions of dollars to help Tea Party candidates win campaigns. And the mass media supported the Tea Party with considerable coverage. The next chapter shows how the people of the Tea Party described in this chapter were not alone. Money and media mattered a lot to the Tea Party and must be understood as critical to the advancement of the movement.

Chapter 4

Tea Party Patrons: Who Has Supported the Movement?

One of the persistent criticisms leveled against the Tea Party has been that it is primarily an "Astroturf" movement, a term credited to Senator Lloyd Bensten (TX) that refers to a political movement that is artificial and top-down, rather than authentically growing up from local communities or "grassroots" in nature. Speaking on his MSNBC show in August 2010, Keith Olbermann opined: "Things go better with Koch—big oil giant Koch Industries that is. Dad created the Astroturf John Birch Society to harass President Kennedy. Now his sons helped create the Astroturf Tea Party to harass President Obama."[1] In Chapter 2, I argued that many of the newly formed Tea Party organizations were not consistent with this image or at least not consistent with such a neat explanation of the origins of the movement. On the contrary, the formation of hundreds of organizations in just a few months in 2009 occurred primarily at the local level, most of these organizations were only weakly tied to national organizations, and few received any financial resources from outside their community. The Roanoke Tea Party was just one example of such an organization with few of the signs of the Astroturfing that Olbermann and others suggested. While pundits have been mixed in their opinions, Skocpol and Williamson argued: "The relationship between big national funders and small grass-roots groups appears to be one of mutual convenience, with little shared knowledge or joint investment, particularly when it comes to Tea Party Express."[2]

However, there is a significant dimension of the Tea Party that does resemble what we would expect from an "Astroturf" movement. I've already touched on certain of those dimensions, particularly the formation and operations of some of the national Tea Party organizations such as FreedomWorks, and also some Tea Party candidates who benefited from enormous direct and indirect financial support. But the Tea Party movement that started in 2009 also sat on a 40- or 50-year project of ideas. For that, you can go back to the 1980s and funding of conservative programs in law schools and development of an array of legal principles—especially those concerning the advancement of states' rights —connected to the Federalist Society.[3] Or you can look to the creation by the Coors and Scaife Foundations of the free-market and antitax think tank, the Heritage Foundation, in the 1970s.[4] You might even go further back to the work of the Mont Pelerin Society and Chicago school in the 1940s and 1950s that established and then institutionalized a set of libertarian, neoliberal, and antiregulatory economic ideas.[5] Similarly rooted are the racially charged dimensions of the Tea Party's hostility toward immigrants and racial minorities that reach back at least to the John Birch Society and Barry Goldwater in the 1960s.[6]

It is certainly true that political movements of one era rely on the intellectual work of scholars and policy entrepreneurs conducted during earlier eras. And that foundational intellectual work is often financially supported by the same patrons who later support aspects of the political movement. It is undeniable, for example, that the Koch family and certain industries supported the development of many of the ideas and institutions of the Tea Party long before 2009.[7] But the focus of this chapter is after 2009 on the support given to the Tea Party during the first and second phases of the movement. I acknowledge the longer history of the ideas of the Tea Party, but do not aim to rehash the excellent scholarship by political and intellectual historians who have already made this case.

I also seek to distinguish between support for the Tea Party movement and funding of other right-wing movements. The Tea Party shares certain things in common with the evangelical Christian movement or the neoconservative foreign policy movement, but there is a risk in casting too wide a net. As the previous chapters of this book show, the Tea Party itself is more varied than often acknowledged, suggesting that additional efforts to group it with other movements could further obscure the clarity of our understanding. I leave an exploration of how similar the Tea Party is to other conservative movements to other scholars, though there are points at which I break this rule in this chapter.

It is also necessary to approach this dimension of the Tea Party with a great awareness of the larger role of wealth and class in U.S. politics. Class is a defining characteristic of the political system in the United States. Poor people participate in politics at lower rates than the wealthy, particularly when we look at elected office. Nicholas Carnes book, *White-Collar Government*, showed just how pervasive social class is in Washington and other centers of power.[8] He wrote: "No blue-collar worker has ever become president. . . . Every seat on the Supreme Court is filled by a lawyer who graduated from Harvard or Yale. . . . And the median net worth of members of Congress is approximately $1.5 million, roughly nineteen times the median net worth of the American family."[9] And these class distinctions make a difference. Carnes concluded: "The numerical underrepresentation of the working class in our legislatures consequently skews economic policy making outcomes that are more in line with what more privileged Americans want."[10] The role of money and wealth in politics is, thus, pervasive across American politics. The Tea Party is simply an example, albeit an exaggerated one, of how money plays a role in contemporary political movements and electoral politics, and will likely continue to play in the future.

Thus, the aim of this chapter is to draw a clearer picture of the financial and nonfinancial supporters of the Tea Party. The role major patrons played in the Tea Party does not negate the grassroots organizing of thousands of individuals and local activists, but attention must be paid to the outsized influence money has played in certain parts of the first and second phases of the movement. The significant role played by the national media also must be considered in understanding the rise of the Tea Party. These are important factors to consider because they also tell a larger story about the unique point in American political history during which the Tea Party flourished. We can learn a lot about the history of this time period, in general, and the role of money and media in politics, in particular, through the lens of the Tea Party. These lessons can better inform our collective understanding of future political movements, as well as efforts to rein in the potentially harmful role of money and the media in the democracy.

In this chapter, I seek to answer the following questions: Who have been the biggest supporters of the Tea Party? Have there been changes in the ways that support has been funneled from the first to the second phase? And in which ways have that funding and other forms of support advanced the Tea Party movement? Answering these questions has become even more critical, but also more difficult, following the 2010 Supreme Court *Citizens United* decision. That decision increased the ease through which nonprofit organizations of all stripes could fund political and campaign activities, but also further limited what we could know about that campaign spending, because of the continued limitations on federal disclosure laws. With that stated, the chapter aims to clarify what can be quite murky political terrain.

THE KOCH BROTHERS AND THE TEA PARTY

No two individuals have gotten as much attention for their complex relationship to various aspects of the Tea Party as Charles and David Koch, also known as the Koch brothers. The two have been portrayed as a cross between a summer blockbuster supervillain and Uncle Pennybags, the mustachioed antihero of the Monopoly board game. The brothers float atop a sea of energy and chemical businesses worth billions, large charitable foundations, and an array of well-funded political organizations. The complexity of the brothers' relationship to the Tea Party derives from many of the same ambiguities that define American politics in the 21st century. Paths of influence are obscured behind organizations with ambiguous names and few obligations to explain who funds operations. Donations are hidden behind often lax regulations on disclosure and protections provided by the First Amendment. And political strategies are difficult to connect to specific tactics and policy outcomes.

For example, neither of the Koch brothers has ever operated, worked, or served as president of an organization called "Tea Party." In fact, one of the Koch brothers told *New York* magazine reporter, Andrew Goldman, "I've never been to a tea-party event. No one representing the tea party has ever even approached me."[11] Taken at face value, this statement is likely true. For decades, the Koch brothers have donated hundreds of millions of dollars a year to everything from medical research to the ballet. It seems reasonable to assume most requests for their patronage go through advisers and related foundations, not directly to one of the brothers. And it is hard to imagine these two billionaires driving down to attend that first local Tea Party event in Roanoke, Virginia, back in 2009.

But upon closer inspection, there are clear ways that the Koch brothers have helped to finance aspects of the Tea Party, albeit in not always transparent ways. One of the first reasons to suspect this connection is that there are key ideological parallels between the family and many leaders of the Tea Party movement. The Koch brothers have shared with some of the Tea Party leaders a deep commitment to libertarian values and related public policies. In actuality, the family has long had a mixed relationship with the Republican Party, so much so that David Koch had run as the vice -presidential candidate on the Libertarian Party ticket in 1980 against Republican Ronald Reagan and Democrat Jimmy Carter. The brothers' shared ideology, thus, has long run counter to certain strains in the Republican Party, particularly the socially conservative platform of the evangelical Christian wing.

As a result of these ideological leanings of the Koch family, they have been instrumental over the last several decades in funding and serving on the boards of libertarian-oriented organizations, such as the Cato Institute.[12] The Cato Institute has been one of the chief intellectual and policy vehicles for libertarian issues, such as advancing market-based policy solutions, reducing environmental regulations, and promoting school choice, since the early 1980s. The organization remained largely nonpartisan in its work for most of its history, mirroring the work of other Washington think tanks such as Brookings and the Urban Institute.[13] Today, Cato explains its mission as

dedicated to the principles of individual liberty, limited government, free markets and peace. . . . Founded in 1977, Cato owes its name to Cato's Letters, a series of essays published in 18th-century England that presented a vision of society free from excessive government power. Those essays inspired the architects of the American Revolution. And the simple, timeless principles of that revolution—individual liberty, limited government, and free markets—turn out to be even more powerful in today's world of global markets and unprecedented access to information than Jefferson or Madison could have imagined. Social and economic freedom is not just the best policy for a free people, it is the indispensable framework for the future.[14]

If you recall Chapter 1 and also Chapter 2, this mission statement should ring some bells for how similar its language is to many Tea Party organizations. The mission statement for the Tea Party Patriots, for example, bears a very strong resemblance:

What unites the tea party movement is the same set of core principles that brought America together at its founding, that kindled the American Dream in the hearts of those who struggled to build our nation, and made the United States of America the greatest, most successful country in world history. At its root the American Dream is about freedom. Freedom to work hard and the freedom to keep the fruits of your labor to use as you see fit without harming others and without hindering their freedom.[15]

This certainly is no coincidence. The Cato Institute has played a special role for advancing libertarian ideas and for those in the Tea Party with libertarian attachments.

The Cato Institute may have established the language and symbols that were later adopted by the Tea Party, but many of the policy ideas that the Koch-backed Cato Institute has advocated for since the early 1980s were also later incorporated into the policy platforms of Tea Party organizations and candidates. On tax issues, the research funded by Cato "explores the benefits of lower taxes, a significantly reduced federal budget, and less government involvement in market processes." This perspective is almost identical to three of the six principles of the Tea Party Express: reduce the size and intrusiveness of government, stop raising our taxes, and cease out-of-control spending.[16] So the *first* way that the Koch brothers have supported the Tea Party has been intellectual. The intellectual links with the Tea Party flow through certain key think tanks that the Koch brothers established and then have funded for decades. Cato's intellectual leadership on libertarianism created some of the infrastructure of ideas that leaders of the Tea Party could later rely upon to channel the political unrest among Tea Party supporters.

But as the intellectual world of Washington politics has grown increasingly partisan, the Koch brothers have also extended their activities beyond the marketplace of ideas to include electoral politics.[17] Gone are the days when organizations like Brookings and the American Enterprise Institute served only as quasi-academic enterprises focused solely on debating ideas. Think tanks always had loose connections to policymaking, but in the late 1990s and 2000s, there were great shifts in how closely certain think tanks hewed to the policy agendas of the two major political parties, and in how closely the two parties were linked to certain organizations. In the 2000s, organizations, such as the Center for American Progress (CAP), merged the traditions of think tanks with the tools of advocacy, communications, and campaigns.[18] CAP, which described itself as an "action tank," created an associated lobbying wing, the CAP Action Fund, to rapidly integrate policy analysis with an aggressive political agenda. CAP was so effective that many of its policy proposals and key staffers were later incorporated into the Obama White House.[19] Conservative organizations, such as the Heritage Foundation, soon followed suit, rendering the primarily nonpartisan and nonpolitical traditions of think tanks and research organizations a thing of the past.

We can see the Koch brothers adapt to this new policy environment—or perhaps they were the ones who initiated the change—by founding a series of political organizations and building a confusing maze of political influence. Parenthetically, the Koch brothers' increasingly political aims also drove a wedge between them and other more traditionally nonpartisan leaders of the Cato Institute, leading to threats of legal recourse and a brief break in the relationship.[20] This melee did not deter the Koch brothers from pursuing their political interests, though it becomes increasingly difficult to fully map the array of organizations with close and distant ties to the family. It is, however, worth sketching a few of those organizations and the links news reports have substantiated. These connections help to make the case that the Koch brothers have supported the Tea Party movement, just not in the most direct or transparent way.

So, with this in mind, in 1984, the Koch brothers had helped establish an organization called Citizens for a Sound Economy. For much of its tenure, the organization acted like most Washington think tanks, producing policy papers and writing libertarian-oriented opinion pieces for newspapers. But in 2004, the organization split into FreedomWorks (described in Chapter 2) and Americans for Prosperity (AFP). I've already explored the very prominent position FreedomWorks has played as a leader of certain nationally centered aspects of the Tea Party, meaning that the Koch brothers have a direct connection to it as well, but AFP is just as interesting. Once in operations, AFP began to play a part in advancing the policy aims of Citizens for a Sound Economy, but it did so with a much more aggressive political strategy, and after 2009, that strategy was tied to the Tea Party. For example, according to reporting by Jane Mayer of the *New Yorker* magazine, one of the ways that AFP supported the Tea Party was by convening training events. Mayer reported that AFP held an event in Austin, Texas, called Texas Defending the American Dream where "five hundred people attended the summit, which served, in part, as a training session for Tea Party activists in Texas."[21] AFP organizers recognized Tea Party leaders at the event and gave a Tea Party activist named Sibyl West its Blogger of the Year award. According to reporting by Mayer, Americans for Prosperity also provided Tea Party activists with lists of key legislators to target for lobbying. Therefore, in addition to establishing some of the intellectual foundation of the Tea Party, a *second* way that the Koch brothers have supported the Tea Party has been through newer political organizations, such as AFP, that have helped to train and educate Tea Party organizers and activists.

But AFP also began to provide more and more monetary support during election time. The Koch brothers underwrote AFP, but not alone, and many of the families' friends and allies also contributed. AFP received considerable support from a related organization called the Center to Protect Patient Rights (CPPR). CPPR had been run by Sean Noble who, the *New Yorker* magazine reported, had close links to the Koch family.[22] Though (because of its organizational status from the Internal Revenue Service [IRS]) AFP does not have to disclose its donors, the Center for Responsive Politics reported that IRS forms indicated that CPPR gave AFP over $11 million in grants in 2010. Freedom Partners Chamber of Commerce, another pillar of the political operations associated with the Koch brothers, also gave a grant worth $32 million to AFP. A reporter for *Politico* described Freedom Partners Chamber of Commerce as "the Koch brothers' secret bank," giving out organizational grants totaling $250 million in 2012, including a meager $200,000 grant to the Tea Party Patriots and a whopping $115 million to CPPR.[23] Who exactly funds the Freedom Partners Chamber is largely unknown, but much of its leadership team has been employed by various Koch organizations in the past. It seems clear that this is indeed a very windy and gold-paved road.

With the financial backing of the Koch brothers, and others supportive of their agenda, AFP initiated a more focused electoral strategy during the 2000s. AFP aided the Tea Party, but the organization's electoral strategy shifted from the first to the second phase of the movement, potentially because of changing constitutional interpretations of campaign spending. AFP's involvement in elections seems to have been shaped and accelerated by the 2010 *Citizens United* Supreme Court decision. The case pitted Citizens United, a conservative political nonprofit organization, against the Federal Election Commission (FEC). Citizens United planned to air a documentary film that criticized Hillary Clinton within 30 days of the 2008 Democratic primaries in which Clinton was a candidate. Lower courts had ruled that the so-called McCain-Feingold law (also known as the Bipartisan Campaign Reform Act (BCRA) of 2002) restricted Citizens United from doing so. The courts had ruled that the law prevented nonprofit organizations from communications deemed "express advocacy," defined as communications that unambiguously supported one candidate over another. An organization could broadcast advertisements that criticized a candidate, but they were prevented from directly connecting the criticism to voting. That type of campaign communications was restricted to candidates and parties, and federal regulations limited how much any person or company could donate to support those entities directly tied to the election. Nonprofits were also free to engage in other types of non-express advocacy electoral communications until 60 days prior to an election. The courts had ruled that Citizens United was in violation of aspects of both of these provisions of the law.

In 2010, the Supreme Court overturned major aspects of the McCain-Feingold law. The *Citizen United* decision eliminated the "express advocacy" restriction and the 60-day limit. As long as it had not coordinated with the candidate or party, a nonprofit organization could now spend unlimited amounts on electoral communications with no restrictions on what they could say or when they could say it. The court upheld other aspects of the law that required disclosure of advertisement spending, and did not address other restrictions on direct donations to candidates.

For the Koch brothers, and many of their allies, *Citizens United* opened range of new political opportunities. (It did so for liberal, progressive, and moderate political patrons as well.) We can observe some of the differences in electoral spending by AFP before and after the ruling. In 2008, the Center for Responsive Politics showed that direct electoral spending by AFP was under $500,000. By 2010, that amount had nearly tripled to

$1.3 million, and by 2012, AFP had topped $30 million. And these figures are just for campaign spending that focused on candidates; they do not include other unregulated issue-focused spending.

The way AFP spent the money also changed notably. In 2010, Americans for Prosperity spent $1.3 million, almost exclusively in opposition advertisements to Democratic candidates in 42 races (Dan Kapanke (WI) and Jean Schodorft (KS) were the two Republican exceptions). According to data from the Center for Responsive Politics, AFP spent more than $100,000 to oppose Democrats in North Carolina, Ohio, Virginia, Wisconsin, Arkansas, and lesser amounts in other races across the country. Much to the dismay of AFP, two of these Democratic candidates, Mike McIntyre (NC) and Ron Kind (WI), ultimately won. What is most noteworthy for this book is that in all of the 42 races except one (the campaign of Democrat Rush Holt (NJ)), the candidate against whom the AFP was opposing was supported by the Tea Party. While the AFP money was not given directly to Tea Party candidates—donations that were still limited by federal election law—these candidates certainly benefited from rapid-fire advertised attacks on their opposition. For those candidates who won, 32 in total, all of them went on to become a part of the Tea Party Class of 2010. Thus, in addition to supporting the development of Tea Party ideas and the training and education of Tea Party leaders, in the first phase of the movement, a *third* way that the Koch brothers were able to support the Tea Party was through the money AFP, the organization that they helped to found and fund, used to defeat Democratic candidates. The Koch brothers were not the only financial supporters of AFP, and many of these candidates received considerable support from other individuals and organizations, but the pattern of support is unambiguous and the positive results for the first phase of the Tea Party hard to doubt.

The *Citizen United* ruling had some impact on the 2010 election, but was likely issued too late in the campaign for most groups to respond during the first phase of the Tea Party. The real impact occurred during the second phase of the Tea Party and the 2012 election. And we can observe a great shift in the amount of candidate-centered spending and the composition of that spending from the AFP. First, AFP substantially increased the amount of spending in 2012. They gave over $36 million in 2012, a massive increase in just two years. That election was also a presidential election year, and AFP responded with a change in spending strategy. Rather than spending to oppose dozens of Democrats running against Tea Party candidates, AFP focused almost exclusively on opposing President Obama. While AFP spent nearly $1.5 million to oppose Senate candidate Tammy Baldwin (D) in Wisconsin, nearly all of the candidate-focused spending—approximately $34.7 million—went to oppose the president.

For the Tea Party, this meant many of their candidates in the House did not receive the same type of AFP support. With AFP's shift to the presidential race, it was Mitt Romney, not exactly a Tea Party candidate, who was most directly helped. Unlike the first phase of the Tea Party, when AFP devoted so much campaign funding to indirectly helping Tea Party candidates by advertising against their opposition, in the second phase the focus moved away from congressional races.

But the direction of opposition advertising to the president was just one type of electoral expenditure associated with AFP. The Center for Public Integrity found that the group had spent over $122 million in 2012, much of that on issue advertisements during the campaign (issue advertisements are distinguished from other types of advertising because they do not mention a particular candidate or voting decisions) opposing the health care law, a major policy objective of the Tea Party movement.[24] It is difficult to track down exactly how much of that went to buying political advertisements, but ad space gets expensive as an election approaches. In the run-up to the 2010 election, Media Matters reported that Americans for Prosperity bought 10,167 advertisements between August and October, a remarkable number, but also less than the 21,570 advertisements paid for by the U.S. Chamber of Commerce and 15,210 from Crossroads Grassroots Policy Strategies (GPS) (another conservative political organization).[25] AFP ran a range of advertisements, including an issue ad opposing Net neutrality featuring a muscular cartoon FCC bully wearing an American flag hat (see: https://www.youtube.com/watch?v=8IK44Lcla98) and thousands of anti-Obamacare ads featuring individuals explaining the personal harm done by the law (see: https://www.youtube.com/watch?v=Kpjyr1x7mC0).

It is difficult to get an exact count of how much the Koch brothers spent on the 2012 election, but estimates run to the $400 million range.[26] What this suggests is that during the second phase of the movement the Koch brothers supported the Tea Party in a *fourth* way, but that support became less candidate-focused. It appears as though the second phase saw a shift to a single race—for the White House—and much more spending focused on issues that the Koch brothers shared with much of the Tea Party. Individual Tea Party organizations and most candidates did not directly benefit from this support, rather they benefited indirectly through the broad advertising for issues such as opposing the health care law.

At the start of this section of the chapter, I argued that we can understand the Koch brothers as not directly involved in any particular Tea Party organizations, but also fundamentally supportive of the Tea Party movement. In at least four ways, through an often confusing array of channels, the Koch brothers were able to support the ideas, training, and financing of Tea Party organizations and candidates. The Koch brothers, of course, were not alone. Many other intellectual patrons helped create the ideas upon which the Tea Party formed and financial backers donated millions to support Tea Party activists participate in the increasingly expensive campaigns of U.S. politics. The Koch brothers stand out for the magnitude of their support, but also the long tenure and leadership of their political influence. They warrant attention, but not at the expense of understanding how other organizations, individuals, and policy changes have enabled the Tea Party movement to flourish, and also what that might mean for the future.

INDUSTRY SUPPORT FOR THE TEA PARTY

The common perception has been that the bond between the Tea Party and the Koch brothers has also been shared with other corporate leaders. Tea Party organizations have often talked in support of lower regulations and free markets, and against the role of government in the economy, all favored principles of corporate America. Such a reading, though, would be too simplistic and would gloss over the reality of what some in the Tea Party have actually pushed. Certain favored Tea Party policies have, in fact, run counter to corporate interest, forcing a wedge between many industries and Tea Party candidates. Since its earliest days, some activists in the Tea Party have strongly opposed what they call "bank bailouts" provided to the financial sector, farm subsidies that support agricultural interests, and tax credits given to energy companies. As a result, the traditional financial supporters of the Republican Party have not all lined up behind the Tea Party, fearing what fiscal austerity and policy change might mean for the bottom line. As Kim Phillips-Fein wrote: "The split between the Tea Party Republicans and the business groups suggests the limits of the politics of the free market."[27]

We can also see the Koch brothers' tricky relationship with the GOP in the level of support from industry for Tea Party candidates. Many industries have long supported Republican candidates, but the emergence of the Tea Party allows us to look even more deeply into industry preferences and divisions within the Republican Party. Data on campaign spending in 2010 Senate races from the Center for Responsive Politics shows that there have been clear differences between the support given to Tea Party candidates and others in the Republican Party without connections to the Tea Party (see Table 4.1).[28] What seems obvious from these data is that industry largely supported non-Tea Party Republicans with much more lavish spending than Tea Party candidates. Non-Tea Party Republican

Senate candidates received, on average, $132,216 from the communications/electronics industry versus just $30,800 for Tea Party Republicans. It is worth noting that these data do not just reflect primary races where Tea Party and non-Tea Party Republicans faced off. It also does not control for the overall spending on each race. It could be that differences in each Senate race drove these variations, but that seems unlikely or at least a separate point. It appears that the same pattern of differential industry spending holds for other sectors, particularly energy, transportation, and defense. It may be the case that each of these industries aligns with the Tea Party on certain issues, but substantial federal spending and advantageous tax incentives benefit energy, transportation, and defense companies. The orthodox Tea Party stance on cutting federal spending, expressed with often total disregard for which programs would be cut, potentially threatened these industries. The libertarian strain of the Tea Party, embodied by the Koch brothers, which has pushed for open markets and reductions in corporate subsidies, may have pushed industry further toward non-Tea Party Republican candidates. Industry may also skew its funding in order to avoid Tea Party candidates defeating more moderate Republicans in the primary, only to lose to moderate Democrats in the general election. There were notable cases (described in more detail in Chapter 5) where marginal Tea Party candidates, such as Sharon Angle (NV) and Christine O'Donnell (DE), won a Republican primary, but eventually lost to a Democrat. Industry may have increasingly slanted its funding in order to limit this chance. Scott Reed, a political operative for the Chamber of Commerce, the chief lobbying organization of corporate America, summed up the tension in this way in an interview with *Politico*:

If you look at the tea party and who the members of the tea party are, they believe in the Constitution, they believe in free enterprise, they believe in less regulations, less taxes, infrastructure spending. I mean, you go through that agenda, that kind of sounds like the Chamber of Commerce on Main Street. So we think the tea party is a winning part of our coalition. Now, when the tea party gets hijacked by a handful of consultants, we think that's wrong and we're going to stand up.[29]

As with other aspects of the Tea Party detailed in earlier chapters of this book, there have been many myths and generalizations about financial support provided to the movement. Many assert that the Tea Party is simply an Astroturf movement supported by elites. Earlier, I explained why this is not necessarily the case: local organizing dominated the first phase of the movement, most with little assistance from the top. But even the elements of the assertion that are true are more complex than often acknowledged. The Koch brothers have provided aid to the Tea Party, but not in direct

Table 4.1 Sector-Level Differences in Support for Tea Party–Favored Republican Senate Candidates and Republican Senate Candidates Not Part of This Bloc

Sector	Non–Tea Party Republican Total	Tea Party–Favored Republican Total
Agribusiness	$3,169,898	$880,610
Communications/Electronics	$3,040,971	$400,406
Construction	$3,021,416	$851,150
Defense	$1,329,900	$26,890
Energy and Natural Resources	$4,409,742	$610,180
Finance, Insurance, and Real Estate	$16,304,212	$3,126,058
Health	$6,003,051	$1,049,125
Lawyers and Lobbyists	$5,958,368	$830,502
Transportation	$2,642,793	$438,975

Source: Center for Responsive Politics, see: http://www.opensecrets.org/news/2010/10/tea-party-loving-republican-senate/

ways, and certainly not alone. And the financial elite have been far from uniform in their support. Many wealthy donors have vehemently resisted the Tea Party and donated millions of dollars to opposing organizations and candidates. But even within the traditional Republican community of supporters, industry groups, such as the U.S. Chamber of Commerce, have had a mixed relationship with the movement. The evidence presented earlier shows that industry was much more supportive of non-Tea Party Republicans than Tea Party Republicans. For some Tea Party candidates, this was hardly detrimental, since Americans for Prosperity and others had already ponied up. But the variety of sources of financial support and opposition is worthy of considering when we examine the first and second phases of the movement, and also looking ahead to where support will come in the future. I return to this theme in the final chapter of the book.

MASS MEDIA AND THE TEA PARTY

Who has funded aspects of the Tea Party has drawn considerable media attention, but the media itself, broadly defined, has also been a major focus of public and scholarly interest in the Tea Party. Whether it is traditional print or television coverage, cable news, or various newer digital outlets (blogs and social media), the emergence of the Tea Party corresponded with a dynamic period in political media.[30] As progressive groups had in the early 2000s, Tea Party organizations were able to use the growing availability, ease of use, and decreasing costs of digital communications technologies to pursue their own media strategies. Chapter 2 showed the importance of the web for organizing, mobilizing, and publicizing for many Tea Party organizations. It is hard to imagine the speed with which the Tea Party organizations grew in the first phase of the movement without e-mail, Twitter, and the Internet. The Tea Party was, thus, able to direct political messages to its constituents without some of the intermediation faced by earlier political movements.

The mass media also played a part in the story of the Tea Party from the outside. But the extent to which certain media outlets were truly outside and which were inside the movement has been hotly contested. Some contended that conservative media became a powerful partner with the Tea Party, advancing the agenda, sharing information, and helping to raise money. You have to look no further than the fact that Rick Santelli's rant was broadcast on cable news to back that claim. Without the mass audience for the network, and ability to replay the rant ad nauseam on other stations and websites, would activists around the nation be mobilized so quickly? Others, though, concede the fawning coverage from some outlets, but conclude that there was as much anti-Tea Party media coverage from opposing sources such as MSNBC, and that the extent of conservative allegiance with the movement may have been oversold. For one, Santelli appeared on CNBC, not the Fox News Network, even though one could expect to see a repeat of his rant on Fox News in the days, weeks, and months to follow.

If we look at what actually happened, Fox News was the first mass media network to cover the earliest mentions of the Tea Party, before it had even turned into an organizational phenomenon. On the February 19, 2009, broadcast of the popular show hosted by Sean Hannity, Fox News played a clip of Rick Santelli to begin a segment with a member of Congress. One day later, another Fox News host, Glenn Beck, coyly questioned a guest who had mentioned the CNBC clip: "But you're not talking about a tea party?" Hannity, Beck, and others were just getting started at this point, but the immediacy of their attention to the Tea Party is hard to overlook. It is, therefore, clear that Fox News was first, but for how long was it alone and to what extent did the network maintain journalistic standards of impartiality?

One of those leading the charge of criticism of the relationship between Tea Party and Fox News was Media Matters for America, an organization that purports to provide information "illustrating skewed or inadequate coverage of important issues, thorough debunking of conservative falsehoods."[31] Media Matters has been a persistent critic of the Fox News Network and saw the network as unusually integrated with the Tea Party. In particular, Media Matters argued that Fox News was involved, not just in reporting on the Tea Party, but actively encouraging participation and attendance at Tea Party rallies. Media Matters wrote on its website "Fox News has frequently aired segments encouraging viewers to get involved with 'Tea Party' protests across the country" and claimed that the channel "has in dozens of instances provided attendance and organizing information for future protests, such as protest dates, locations and website URLs."[32] Along these lines, the Fox News website collected and published the locations of many of the major Tax Day Tea Party rallies in 2009 under the headline: "Welcome to *FoxNews*' Anti-Tax Tea Party Coverage." The post read: "Just as 18th century decrees by the British drew outrage from American colonists, several acts of modern U.S. government intervention have stirred similar upheaval by taxpayers across the land. *FOX News* will have all the details leading right up to April 15 tax day—from links to tea parties in you [*sic*] area to live reports from the scenes, analyses from the FOX Forum and FOXNews.com's own series of the tea party phenomenon." Media Matters deemed the various aspects of Fox News' coverage of the Tea Party as excessive and not keeping with the standards of unbiased journalism that the network asserts and that viewers of the news have, we hope, continued to expect.

The empirical record from social science researchers in a number of fields yields a more mixed assessment of media support for the Tea Party and the particular role played by Fox News. In general, the case for Fox News presenting a vastly different face for the movement has not been consistently demonstrated with evidence. But because of the attention drawn to political media and the Tea Party, it is worth investigating the substance of that research to understand the role media played in supporting, opposing, and informing the Tea Party. Also, some of the ways conservative media aided the Tea Party may be too subtle and private to uncover using the standard data collection methods of social scientists, but still worthy of further investigation.

Much of the research on the media dimension of the Tea Party comes from the earliest days of the first phase of the movement. For example, Skocpol and Williamson showed a major spike in cable news coverage of the Tea Party.[33] In the run-up to the Tax Day protests in 2009, the frequency of stories about the Tea Party grew from under 50 (on Fox News) in March to ebb at over 200 for both CNN and the Fox News Network on April 12. But CNN's interest in the story flowed following that date, while Fox News continued with a lesser, but still considerable number of stories through the end of May. It is worth reiterating that within the landscape of cable television news, the Fox News Network features a more consistently conservative approach and more conservative commentators, MSNBC delivers an analogous approach on the progressive side, and CNN locates its coverage some place in the middle. Some of these ideological differences manifest in the choices of guests, commentators, and nonnews programming. While the magnitude of the ideological leaning of cable news can be debated, the common impression is that differences exist. As such, Skocpol and Williamson concluded that "Fox [News Network] was not just responding to the Tea Party activism as it happened. Fox served as a kind of social movement orchestrator, during what is always a dicey early period for any new protest effort. . . . For weeks in advance of each early set of rallies, as the Tea party grew from infancy to adolescences, *Fox* was pointing the way and cheering."[34]

Later in the first phase, as the 2010 election approached, other networks began to pick up the Tea Party story. Jules Boykoff and Eulalie Laschever's research continued where Skocpol and Williamson left off.[35] The election of 2010 was the inflection point between the first and second phase of the Tea Party, and it also was the evening of most concentrated news coverage of the Tea Party. On that night, news outlets referred to the Tea Party nearly as often as they did the president, whose Democratic allies in the House were facing stinging midterm defeats. According to research on news coverage on the major television networks and cable stations conducted by the Pew Research Center, much of the coverage also interpreted the election outcome as a sign of success for the Tea Party. While the largest fraction, a quarter of coverage, framed the election as a "GOP rout," 18% argued that the election was a success for the Tea Party and only 11% as a setback for the movement. This is another indicator that the tone of coverage for the Tea Party during the first phase was positive, but not necessarily because Fox News was the only network framing the story, but other outlets also concurred.

Most of the previously published work on this issue has been from the first phase of the movement. Some of these patterns persisted through the second, but changes were also evident. In order to examine this, I reconstructed the approximate method used by Skocpol and Williamson to make their claims about the leading role played by Fox News, but I extended the data collection through the summer of 2014, far into the second phase of the movement.[36] I also compared the coverage of Fox News with MSNBC, rather than with CNN. This is in part to address the claims of conservative bias, but also because the data maintained on CNN coverage are much more extensive than other cable news networks; therefore we can get a skewed impression of their prominence. Fox News and MSNBC are natural competitors and worthy of a direct comparison.

In Figure 4.1, we can observe a variety of trends and patterns of cable news coverage of the Tea Party. During the first phase, as has been previously demonstrated, Fox News clearly covered the Tea Party much more extensively than MSNBC. The volume of coverage during the first phase first peaked at the Tax Day protest, when Fox News broadcast four times as many stories that mentioned the Tea Party compared to MSNBC. One year later, in April 2010, coverage again spiked for both networks, and again Fox News coverage was considerably higher than for MSNBC. Finally, as the critical 2010 election approached, both networks increased coverage, but around Election Day 2010, Fox News hit new heights for coverage of the Tea Party during the first phase. Much as Skocpol and Williamson and other researchers have demonstrated, media coverage during the first phase of the Tea Party tracked with major events, including protests and elections. The first phase was also dominated by Fox News coverage to a much greater extent than one of its chief competitors, MSNBC.

Figure 4.1 also reveals new information about the second phase of the Tea Party movement and extends what previous researchers have demonstrated in the past. First, coverage spiked at the start of the second phase. The combined coverage from MSNBC and Fox News in August 2011 was higher than at any other point in the second phase. During August, major Republican presidential candidates spoke at a number of Tea Party events, drawing considerable media attention. Second, while Fox News continued to cover the Tea Party, following the August 2011 peak, there was a considerable decline in the network's coverage. From March 2012 through May 2013, the Fox News Network provided only limited coverage of the Tea Party, and only later that year increased its coverage. Third, the election in 2012, unlike the election in 2010, spurred much less coverage of the

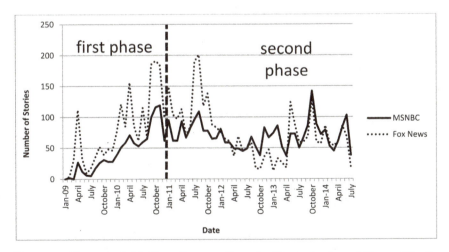

Figure 4.1 Change in Cable News Coverage from the First to the Second Phase of the Tea Party (Original data collection using Lexis-Nexis)

Tea Party across the board, and particularly from Fox News. This change tracks nicely, though not causally, with an analogous shift in campaign spending from Tea Party candidates in 2010 to opposing the president in 2012. Fourth, and perhaps most significantly, the second phase of the movement saw the emergence of MSNBC in Tea Party coverage. Largely absent from the first phase, MSNBC took over the lead during 2012, continually covering the Tea Party to a much greater extent than Fox News. For example, during the 2012 election, MSNBC provided approximately double the amount of coverage for the Tea Party than Fox News, a reversal of what had happened in 2010.

The empirical record on the volume of media coverage of the Tea Party suggests a shift from the first to the second phase of the movement. Fox News was the initial leader, but MSNBC later took over as the primary source of Tea Party coverage. These are interesting findings, but only tell a portion of the story. If we believe viewers chose to watch the two networks randomly, watched both networks with equal frequency, or the two networks provided the same type of coverage, then quantifying coverage would tell us nearly all of what we need to know. However, there is ample evidence that this is not the case. As Chapter 2 showed, viewers sort themselves by network—conservatives with Fox News and progressives with MSNBC—and the two networks seem to have different perspectives on how to cover the news. Skocpol and Williamson asserted that the dominant tone of media coverage of the earliest part of the first phase of the movement was driven by the positive tone set by Fox News. Since it was providing the most coverage, there was less information available from other sources, including the more neutral CNN and more skeptical MSNBC. Many other scholars have been interested in verifying these claims to see whether the coverage of the Tea Party, such as the Election Night coverage, differed by news outlet. One of the reasons for such interest in this is what we know about the viewing habits of Americans. As I showed in Chapter 2, in the increasingly polarized politics of the country, evidence suggests that news consumers seek out different news based on their partisan affiliations and ideological leanings. Generally speaking, strident conservatives spend an inordinate amount of time watching Fox News, while passionate liberals restrict their watching to MSNBC. As such, it reasons that news coverage of the Tea Party might differ from station to station, potentially reinforcing and emboldening the beliefs of supporters and opponents of the Tea Party.

The research by Boykoff and Laschever pursued this line of inquiry.[37] They showed that as the election neared, the composition of who was reporting on the Tea Party shifted. CNN became the primary source of news stories about the movement, followed by Fox News and the more liberal-leaning MSNBC. But as other news outlets got into the game of covering the Tea Party, we can begin to observe more variation in how the Tea Party was covered. Media scholars use the term "framing," "themes," or "paradigms" to refer to the angle or direction of a news story. Frames provide a narrative structure to a set of facts, and allow the news consumer to better connect those facts to other ideas. Boykoff and Laschever compared coverage in terms of whether it used a positive "grassroots" frame or a negative "establishment" frame. Some news outlets, including ABC and the *New York Times*, balanced coverage between the two frames, while others favored one frame or the other. Most outlets, including CNN, CBS, Fox News, *USA Today*, and the *Wall Street Journal*, all used the grassroots frame to a greater extent than the establishment frame. Only MSNBC highlighted the establishment frame much more often than the grassroots frame. Research by Anthony DiMaggio concurred with Boykoff and Laschever in his analysis that "mass media outlets frame the Tea Party very positively across the board. . . . Closer analysis of reporting on the Tea Party show they adopt a sympathetic line toward the group, similar to, but less blatant than that seen in right-wing media."[38] This evidence comports with the suggestion that Fox News supported a positive image of the Tea Party, but that approach was far from anomalous. In fact, it was MSNBC's coverage that departed to the greatest extent from the conventional news wisdom about the Tea Party.

Others have further examined the question of Fox News coverage. Damon DiCiccio and Colin Lingle compared framing by cable news outlets using either a pro—what they operationalize as framing the Tea Party using optimistic, patriotic, or "national rhetoric"—or generally skeptical—what they operationalize as framing the Tea Party as a "nuisance" or covering just the "protest" aspects of the movement.[39] While they found slight differences in terms of negative framing, Fox News was less likely to focus on the negative "protest paradigm," but there was little difference between Fox News and MSNBC in terms of the positive "national rhetoric." Fox News, MSNBC, and CNN all used the "nuisance paradigm" to the same extent. DiCiccio and Lingle concluded: "We see that all three channels—including both MSNBC and Fox News—used national rhetoric frequently and in comparable ways, but Fox offered significantly less protest paradigm coverage of the Tea Party protests."[40] Again, in terms of framing, there is limited evidence that Fox News coverage was significantly different in framing than other cable news stations.

A related concern among those in the Tea Party was whether the media was undermining the movement through dismissive coverage. One research paper addressed this issue by looking at whether there were differences in how cable news stations used frames to *delegitimize* the Tea

Party. David Weaver and Joshua Sacco studied news coverage that referred to the Tea Party as made up of "idiots" and references to the movement's colorful attire, language that would undermine the legitimacy of the Tea Party movement.[41] They found that MSNBC was the most likely to use the language of delegitimization and also the most likely to claim that the Tea Party was primarily an Astroturf movement. The differences in news coverage, again, were driven as much by Fox News as by the direction of MSNBC's coverage.

To find that there were differences in media coverage of the Tea Party is not the same as the finding that coverage was inaccurate or dishonest. As this book has made efforts to show, the Tea Party can be many things to many different people, at once a parade of old men in colonial costume and at the same time a serious examination of the vitality of country's protection of personal liberty. While some claimed coverage distorted their view of the movement, there was evidence that Tea Party organizers believed news coverage was generally fair. The *Washington Post* conducted a survey of local Tea Party organizers and asked them about how fair the coverage was of their group. Over three-quarters of respondents (76%) said that coverage was either fair or somewhat fair, and just 8% found coverage "very unfair."[42] Again, the wild claims of grossly distorted coverage and media dishonesty about the Tea Party are not fully supported with the empirical evidence.

Most of the research on the Tea Party and the media focuses on the visible, accessible forms such as television, radio, or newspapers. But the role of the media in advancing the Tea Party also had a more hidden aspect. One way that the Tea Party and media worked together was in the form of sponsored content. Dick Armey, the former chair of FreedomWorks, explained how the organization spent millions of dollars to have conservative radio hosts, Rush Limbaugh and Glenn Beck, promote Tea Party events and help fund-raising. Armey was so dismayed by these expenditures that he resigned from the organization shortly after discovering these contracts.[43] What is most intriguing about this type of media support for the Tea Party is that while it appears to be a part of regular radio programming, not an advertisement, the reality is that it is sponsored. A report in the magazine, *Mother Jones*, cited an internal FreedomWorks document that referred to spending on "embedded media programs." The organization's 2013 budget called for spending on "Glenn Beck Radio Ads," "Glenn Beck TV," and "Rush Limbaugh Contract."[44] So, in theory, what happens is that in addition to whatever commentary Glenn Beck or Rush Limbaugh chose to offer on the Tea Party, the sponsored content contract would guarantee that they would also add references to opportunities to support Tea Party organizations and attend Tea Party events. The FreedomWorks document credited "Beck" with generating $859,099 and "Rush" with $433,484 in revenue, presumably from donations that could be tracked back to the sponsorship arrangements. This element of the media's role in the Tea Party must be accounted for in a full assessment of the progress of the movement.

Overall, research suggests that the media widely covered the Tea Party, particularly at key moments during the first phase, Tax Day 2009 and Election Day 2010. The Fox News Network began covering the movement first, but others soon followed, particularly CNN. News coverage provided support for the Tea Party by spreading the emergence of Tea Party groups, the location of protests, and key messages. The evidence suggests that the Fox News Network was somewhat more supportive than other outlets, but that the extent of the difference in coverage has been exaggerated. Fox News Network featured slightly more positive frames and significantly fewer negative frames compared to MSNBC.

Less clear, however, is the extent to which some coverage by conservative media personalities was genuinely a part of their coverage of the news aspects of the Tea Party and what part was the result of sponsored agreements. At least some of what listeners to conservative radio heard about the Tea Party was directly tied to FreedomWorks. This programming was used to generate support for the Tea Party and raise funds for the organization. The increasing reliance on this type of arrangement undermines claims by those in the Tea Party that it was solely a grassroots organic movement and buffers the claims of Astroturfing. Measuring the extent of this aspect of media coverage, though, remains difficult.

What does seems clear from the evidence is that the growth of the Tea Party could not have happened in the way it did without the mass mobilization made possible by various media outlets. Whether genuine or false, the media played a critical role in elevating and supporting the Tea Party movement.

CONCLUSION

Previous chapters of this book showed that hundreds of Tea Party organizations formed within a few months of Rick Santelli's 2009 rant on CNBC. Organizations formed in the cities and towns, across states, and in important national centers of politics. At the same time, individuals across the country were drawn to the exciting message of the Tea Party, the symbols of Americana, and the opportunity to participate in a new social movement that expressed their beliefs. There are many reasons to believe the organizational activists and supporters of the Tea Party had genuine political beliefs and expressed their interests in a forthright fashion. Aspects of the Tea Party were truly grassroots.

Preceding Rick Santelli's rant, though, was decades of active policy entrepreneurship. Since the 1950s, intellectuals have been building the ideas and institutions that sit as the foundation of the Tea Party. They have been aided by patrons who have given hundreds of millions of dollars to advance these intellectual projects. More recently, because of changing political norms and regulations, these efforts have taken a much more political turn. Instead of a long-term strategy focused on the marketplace of ideas and institution building, patrons have adopted a short-term strategy of elections. Thus, there were also aspects of the Tea Party that resembled an Astroturf movement, dominated by political elites.

We can observe a bit of this change in elite strategy in microcosm during the first two phases of the Tea Party. The first phase of the Tea Party was mostly, though not exclusively, focused on heated discussions of the ideas of liberty at rallies and protests as well as the formation of organizations so that individuals could participate in this conversation. Much of the effort of the first phase was thus placed on planning local events, designing websites, and writing mission statements. The second phase, though, saw a sharp shift in strategy and tactics. Major patrons, like the Koch brothers, increasingly saw the Tea Party as a vehicle within which it could advance a short-term strategy. It appears as though the local and organizational dimension of the Tea Party became secondary to a multimillion-dollar strategy to oppose Democratic congressional candidates and support those affiliated with the Tea Party. And later, this strategy further shifted to an even more centralized financial strategy focused almost exclusively against President Obama and the new national health care law. In this chapter we saw that shift reflected in the ways major patrons greatly increased funding from 2008 to 2012, but also in the way they spent money. Thus, the Tea Party has been supported by national financial elites, but in several different ways. Prior to 2009, the Tea Party was supported by the intellectual groundwork to legitimize libertarian and conservative ideas and policy proposals. Tea Party activists could not have advanced a coherent policy strategy without this work over earlier decades. After 2009, during the first phase, the Tea Party was supported by some of the national organizations that had been established by patrons like the Koch brothers. Freedom-Works and Americans for Prosperity were just two organizations that helped Tea Party activists across the country learn how to organize, mobilize, and participate in politics. After the 2010 election, during the second phase, the Tea Party was supported through the newly elected members of Congress, many of whom owed their electoral success to the Koch brothers. Without the massive increase in political advertising during the 2010 election that targeted certain Democrats with Tea Party opposition, the Tea Party would likely not have ended up with as much power in Congress.

But the Tea Party was also supported by other sources of power. The growing influence of mass media in politics, particularly the increasingly polarized and partisan nature of cable news, played a major part in the advancement of the movement. Without the coverage provided by the Fox News Network in the early days of 2009, it is likely that many fewer people would have ever heard of Rick Santelli's rant or this idea of a modern Tea Party. It seems that Fox News Network drew attention to the growing movement, to protests and rallies, and to opportunities to join and donate to Tea Party organizations. The rapid increase in support and organization growth likely could not have happened with as much speed if Fox News Network had not paid such close attention.

But similar to the help of financial patron, mass media support for the Tea Party also shifted from the first to the second phase of the movement. The first phase was clearly dominated by Fox News coverage. Original research presented in this chapter verifies what other scholars have found previously for the volume of coverage. But arguments about bias remain. Much of the empirical research finds only minor differences between the tone and substance of Fox News coverage versus other networks. Fox News may have given the Tea Party a lot of air time, but it does not appear as though that coverage emphasized the patriotism of activists any more than CNN or other traditional television networks. In fact, some research shows that the greatest differences in coverage of the Tea Party came from MSNBC. MSNBC was more likely to use delegitimizing frames during its Tea Party coverage than other news outlets. This finding is even more interesting when we look to what happened in the second phase. MSNBC, which had remained relatively inactive during the first phase, became much more focused on the Tea Party during the second phase. This shift, combined with the negative tone of much of its coverage, occurred at the same time public opinion toward the Tea Party began to wane. Commentators have pinned causal arguments on findings like these, and have suggested that Fox News propped up the Tea Party with unfairly positive coverage and MSNBC has dampened interest with its equally negative coverage. Causation is exceedingly difficult to demonstrate in a circumstance like this. Since we know viewers sort themselves by ideology and political interest, the relationship between cable network coverage and the level of support or opposition for the Tea Party is likely just a correlation. Strong Tea Party supporters grew in excitement along with Fox News during the first phase of the Tea Party. Nonsupporters were likely unaware of the details of the movement during the first phase, since they probably were not intently watching Fox News. But as Tea Party candidates won in 2010, natural opponents awoke, formed much more negative opinions, and were watching MSNBC at the same time.

The role of outside supporters of the Tea Party is both complex and deeply rooted in the political times. The new century has increasingly been defined by the growing role of money in politics and campaigns. It has also been defined by the role of mass media, new ways to collect political information, and also the polarization of news. The story of the Tea Party illustrates these trends in numerous ways that make the movement a fascinating case study to understand modern politics.

Chapter 5

Tea Party Legislators: Evaluating the Class of 2010 and Beyond

The Tea Party began with the rapid organizing of thousands of people who believed in an array of ideas, including fiscal austerity, lower taxes, and stronger immigration laws. While previous chapters of this book showed that both the organizations and the people were more varied than we may have acknowledged, the Tea Party was defined by these two aspects of the movement. Organizing and people made up the most dynamic aspects of the first phase of the movement, in part, because up until that point, there was almost nobody who could claim to have won an election as a Tea Party candidate (the Tea Party Caucus was formed in 2010 before the election, but it was initially made up of members of Congress who had campaigned prior to the rise of the Tea Party). Those who made up the movement remained political outsiders during the first phase.

But as the country approached the fall 2010 congressional election, the Tea Party movement went from a primarily outsider, renegade movement, made up of organizations and people to one contending for actual political power and increasingly represented by elected members of Congress. Much as the foundation of the Democratic Party was remade in 1968 by the New Left movement, the second phase of the Tea Party movement witnessed the center of the Republican Party continue to shift rightward.[1] Candidates for office ran under the mantle of the Tea Party, many claiming to share the values of Tea Party supporters, and promising to represent those values in Washington. Tea Party groups endorsed, supported, and campaigned for some of these candidates, often in opposition to an incumbent or an establishment Republican candidate. While some suffered at the ballot box, other Tea Party candidates were successful and followed a wave of Republican success in the House and Senate. Thus, the second phase of the movement, which began after the 2010 election, must be understood in terms of those who were elected, how they legislated, and the differences between those who affiliated with the Tea Party. But the shift to electoral politics did not happen easily for all parts of the Tea Party. Electoral politics invited disagreements and dissension in certain parts of the country as individuals stood to gain from winning office, and others to lose. The second phase also saw Tea Party candidates challenge long-standing Republican officials, thereby driving a wedge between the movement and others who shared some of their beliefs.

For example, if we return back to Roanoke, Virginia, and the Roanoke Tea Party described in Chapter 2, we see how electoral politics divided the Tea Party in the state. Local Tea Party organizations across Virginia had formed a statewide federation of Tea Party groups. The federation planned a convention in the summer of 2011 to share policy ideas and discuss the future of the movement in the state and elsewhere. Greg Aldridge and his Roanoke Tea Party colleagues helped plan the convention, contributed money, and encouraged attendance from their ranks. They also came to the convention in the state capital, Richmond, with a specific strategy to regain power from the federal government, an original principle of the Tea Party movement.

The idea, called "nullification," has a long history in American political thought that stretches back to the formation of the country. The essential concept, originally articulated by Thomas Jefferson and James Madison, is that states have a constitutional right to reject, or nullify, any law passed by the federal government that it deems unconstitutional. Nullification was used in some southern states to resist federal efforts in the 1950s to desegregate public schools.[2] The Roanoke Tea Party believed that Virginia could use nullification to promote state control over public policy. As such, leaders wrote a piece of sample legislation called the "Freedom for Virginians Act," which they hoped others in the Virginia federation would consider supporting.

Organizers of the state convention granted the group from Roanoke time to present their idea, but that time was slowly whittled down from 20 minutes, to 15, to 10, and finally to 7 minutes squeezed between performances of the country band hired for the event. The Roanoke Tea Party slowly lost its speaking time, in part, because its leaders believed they were provoking the leader of the Richmond Tea Party and chair of the statewide federation, Jamie Radtke. Radtke, and others, shared the Roanoke Tea

Party's concern about unchecked federal power, but supported an alternative strategy focused on amending the federal constitution, the "Repeal Amendment." The Repeal Amendment would allow two-thirds of state legislators to repeal any federal law. The objectives of the nullification bill and this constitutional amendment might be similar for Virginia, but the political strategy was quite different: one focused just on the state and the other on a national effort.

But Radtke also had set her sights on elected office. Leaders of the Roanoke Tea Party believed that Radtke planned to use the convention to debate the Republican nominee for open Senate seat in the state, former governor George Allen. George Allen was popular in the state, but deemed too moderate and not sufficiently responsive to the values of the Tea Party to garner widespread support. The Roanoke Tea Party believed Radtke would use the proceedings of the convention debate, and questionable statements made by Allen, to launch her own campaign. At the time, Radtke had not yet announced her candidacy, but the Roanoke Tea Party leaders came to see the convention as an event planned to support her forthcoming campaign, rather than as a forum to discuss issues like nullification. While not a candidate during the convention, shortly after it ended, Radtke announced her candidacy, and ultimately challenged Allen and the Democrat, Tim Kaine, who ultimate won the Senate race.

But the conflict between the Roanoke Tea Party and statewide leaders, such as Jamie Radtke, did not end at the conclusion of the convention, nor did it remain focused on political strategy. The Roanoke Tea Party's vocal dissent and criticism of the mixed motivations of Radtke incensed leaders of the federation. On a federation conference call shortly after the convention ended, a vote was called and the Roanoke Tea Party was narrowly voted out of the federation. According to Greg Aldridge, "We got kicked out of the federation when the convention was over. They got a majority of votes together to vote against us, to throw us out, seven voted with us." It remains unclear whether it was the dustup over the nullification bill or questions the organization raised about Radtke's electoral ambition, but Aldridge maintained that "they didn't follow the rules . . . in the by-laws of the federation there is a specific list of offenses for the leadership to vote people out, we broke none of those."

Such is the nature of a political movement that evolves from grassroots organizing to campaign politics. Much of the unity, energy, and consensus that can drive the early stages of a political movement like the Tea Party soon dissipates as individuals seek out their political fortunes in state capitals and Washington, D.C. Later stages of a movement often see parties enveloping movement leaders and restraining much of the movement's energy, as Michael Heaney and Fabio Rojas (2014) showed for the antiwar movement and the Democratic Party in 2000s.[3] Political campaigns open new opportunities to advance policy goals, but also expose new challenges. The plight of the Roanoke Tea Party that ran afoul of the increasingly complicated politics of the second phase of the Tea Party illustrates these challenges.

I first examine the Tea Party candidates of 2010, and then the ways those who were electorally successful ultimately legislated. I also analyze the way national organizations made candidate endorsements in 2012. In doing so, I show that the second phase of the Tea Party movement, now centered in Washington, features new ways to understand the changing politics of the Tea Party.

WHAT DID IT MEAN TO BE A TEA PARTY CANDIDATE IN 2010?

As the earlier chapters of this book show for other features of the movement, defining the pool of Tea Party candidates for elected office is tricky: should we count only first-time candidates with formal ties to Tea Party organizations? Or should incumbents who share values with the Tea Party also be counted? Estimates range greatly, but some of the most reliable analysts suggested that there were as many as 140 Tea Party congressional candidates in 2010: 10 running in the Senate and 130 for seats in the House of Representatives. This does not count those congressional incumbents who had joined the Congressional Tea Party Caucus formed by Michele Bachman (R-MN) in March 2010.

Where Tea Party candidates competed also varied greatly, such that there were candidates running for Congress in 34 different states, including solidly blue states such as New York, Oregon, and Illinois. Some of the most notable Tea Party campaigns were in Nevada, Colorado, and Texas, where Tea Party candidates defeated incumbent or establishment Republican candidates in party primaries. The surprising primary defeats of long-serving Congressman Mike Castle (DE) by Christine O'Donnell (who eventually lost the Senate race) and Senator Bob Bennett (UT) by Mike Lee (who eventually won the Senate seat) were particularly notable.

In the Senate, Pat Toomey (PA), Rand Paul (KY), Marco Rubio (FL), Ron Johnson (WI), and Mike Lee (UT) all won, while Christine O'Donnell (DE), Sharon Angle (NV), John Raese (WV), Ken Buck (CO), and Joe Miller (AK) all lost. Many of these Senate losses defined the 2010 election because Democrats won high-profile races in Delaware, Nevada, and Colorado that the party was initially expected to lose.

Summarizing the success of the Tea Party depends on how you count wins and losses, whether you count primary wins and losses, and who exactly is in the pool. Jonathan Mummolo offered an interesting comparison of various Tea Party success rates by endorsements.[4] FreedomWorks, Tea Party Express (TPE), and others made endorsements of Tea Party candidates in 2010. FreedomWorks endorsed 113 House candidates, TPE endorsed 138 House candidates, and Sarah Palin endorsed 32 House candidates. Each powerful force behind the Tea Party had different rates of endorsement success. FreedomWorks had the highest success rate: 72 of the 113 (64%) endorsed candidates won. TPE endorsed 85 winning candidates out of a total of 138 (62%). Sarah Palin chose right in 19 of her 32 endorsements (59%). In the Senate, the endorsement success rate was lower: 10 of 21 FreedomWorks endorsed candidates won (48%); 9 of 17 TPE endorsed candidates won (53%); and 5 of 9 Palin endorsed candidates won (56%). Interestingly, Mummolo cautioned against drawing a causal conclusion about the influence of these Tea Party organizations. He explained that FreedomWorks, at least, made endorsements based in part on who it thought would win, suggesting that it did not endorse candidates who were too far down in the preelection polls.

In the House of Representatives, the Tea Party's success rate was similar to the Senate, but we can observe more geographic variation because of the larger total number of candidates. For example, in Florida three of the four Tea Party candidates won; and in Illinois four of the eight won. In South Carolina, Tea Party candidates won four elections, and thus made up more than half of the state's seven-seat delegation. But in California, there were 16 Tea Party candidates and not one was victorious. In North Carolina, much more hospitable to Tea Party candidates, only one of five candidates, Renee Elmers, won a seat in the House.

Another group interested in the Tea Party candidates was the national advocacy organization, the Club for Growth. The Club, for example, assigned 87 successful candidates for the House of Representatives with the Tea Party label, what it dubbed "The Tea Party Class of 2010." I use the Club for Growth list to analyze the group of successful Tea Party candidates later in this chapter. As noted earlier, precise counting is problematic for the Tea Party, but different estimates seem to agree that the electoral success of the Tea Party was far from overwhelming. Moreover, there is a certain irony of Tea Party victories. For those candidates who ended their campaigns in 2010 with a victory, they won the right to work in the city that had served as a foil for many of their campaigns. So many Tea Party candidates had used Washington as the symbol of all that was wrong with the country. The great irony of the second phase of the Tea Party movement is that the geographic focus of so much of the ire of the first phase was exactly where the successful Tea Party candidates landed. Once in Washington, the Tea Party movement had to confront the reality, difficulty, and complexity of actual power.

But candidates are elected as individuals, therefore it is important to focus on the individual characteristics of those Tea Party candidates who won. It is also important to focus on individuals because individual candidate backgrounds varied. Thus, it is worth focusing on a semirandom sampling of a few of these successful candidates in 2010: Raul Labrador (R-ID), Justin Amash (R-MI), Vicky Jo Hartzler (R-MO), and David McKinley (R-WV).

RAUL LABRADOR

Republican candidate Raul Labrador used the myth of the Tea Party to campaign for office, but he also exemplified many aspects of another national myth: that of the American Dream. As such, Labrador's path to Congress was hardly as an outsider or revolutionary; he fit with what we have come to expect from members of Congress, at least in the most mythical fashion. Labrador was born in Puerto Rico, but his family relocated to Las Vegas, Nevada, as a child. A converted Mormon, he later attended college in Utah and did missionary work abroad before returning home. He then earned a law degree in Seattle, Washington, before setting up a legal practice in Idaho.

As many ambitious lawyers are wont to do, Labrador then turned to politics. He successfully ran for the Idaho House of Representatives in 2006, and then had a surprise victory for the seat in the U.S. House of Representatives in 2010 as a Tea Party candidate. Labrador won his seat in Congress on a Tea Party–friendly platform of cutting taxes, advancing pro-life legislation, enhancing border security, and protecting gun rights. He also was endorsed by the National Rifle Association, National Right to Life, as well as the infamous anti-immigration Arizona sheriff, Joe Arpaio. But Labrador's victory was far from expected. His Republican primary opponent, Vaughn Ward, was heavily supported by the National Republican Party and even by Tea Party favorite, Sarah Palin.[5] Labrador faced off with Ward, equipped with few of the resources provided to his opponent and as a potential threat to the national Republican establishment.

In the end, though, it may have been the fact that Labrador gained a late endorsement from the 2,500-person strong, Tea Party Boise, which ultimately swung the election in his favor.[6] This state Tea Party organization provided some of the ground support needed to challenge Labrador's own party's favored candidate, and then the Democrat in the general election. Indicative of a path to Congress that ran *around* the Republican Party rather than *with* it, Labrador later explained how he understood the Tea Party:

What people don't understand about the Tea Party, the Tea Party didn't arise because of President Barack Obama. The Tea Party arose because they were frustrated with the Republican Party. These were people who had been disaffected with Republicans for eight years, and they were silent because they thought, "I can't talk bad about my Republican brethren." But after they saw President Barack Obama elected, they said: "We should have said something before. We should have said something in 2004. We should have said something in 2006." And that's why you saw the level of frustration because they had been quiet for so long, and all of a sudden they erupted. They couldn't believe what they were seeing.[7]

This framing of the Tea Party movement helps to make sense of Labrador's election and his later moves to unseat longtime Republican members in the House leadership. But in other ways, Labrador's background is quite conventional. There is perhaps no better model for the American Dream than the path Labrador traveled from newcomer to law school to Congress. Labrador brought that background to Congress in 2010, but also a strongly conservative view of immigration, favoring a law that would make English the national language and opposing reforms that would provide a path to citizenship for undocumented individuals.[8] But while many in the Tea Party expressed a strong identity as political outsiders, Labrador followed many of the steps common to American politicians for two hundred years.

JUSTIN AMASH

Justin Amash shared aspects of Congressman Labrador's personal and professional story, but was born and raised in the midwestern state of Michigan, and reflected the ethnic roots of his region of the state. Amash's is a second-generation Arab American, but his religious background is Christian not Muslim, which made him similar to many first- and second-generation immigrants in Michigan. Amash attended college and law school, and later ran successfully for the Michigan House of Representatives on a strongly libertarian platform.

Several years later, in 2010, Amash was one of the youngest candidates for national office. At just 30, Amash ran for the open seat of retiring Congressman Vern Ehlers in a competitive Republican primary. Drawn to his libertarian ideals, Amash was endorsed by TPE and other local Tea Party groups in Michigan. With the support of the Tea Party, Amash won the Republican nomination, and later defeated the Democratic candidate in the general election with 60% of the vote, becoming one of the few Arab American members of Congress.

Amash and Labrador both won as Tea Party candidates, but neither was an unusual candidate for office. They were both attorneys with considerable legislative experience prior to seeking national office. Yet, both also differed from the conventional notions of the identity of the Tea Party. Neither was white and neither was particularly old compared to other members of Congress. While each may have represented largely white and older Tea Party voters, they each brought a level of diversity to Congress that departs from the expectations many have built about the movement based on the demographics of Tea Party supporters during its first phase.

VICKY JO HARTZLER

Vicky Jo Hartzler's path to national politics was a little less conventional than Labrador or Amash; she was trained and worked as a home economics teacher for 11 years, rather than cutting her teeth in the law. Hartzler's sex and her educational background made her distinct in the Tea Party, but she too had sought out a political life in state politics with a successful run for the House of Delegates in Missouri in 2000. She won on a socially conservative platform that featured her opposition to gay marriage.

After a brief time away, she returned to politics to run for the House of Representatives in 2010 against longtime Democrat, Ike Skelton. Hartzler was endorsed by conservative groups, including Gun Owners of America, as well as by Sarah Palin. During the campaign, Hartzler appeared at a Tea Party meeting and later said to the local newspaper, the *St. Louis Beacon*: "The Fourth District has been Tea Party in its philosophy since before the Tea Party existed. We just think it is mainstream to want to have a budget that balances, to rein in runaway federal spending, and to lower the tax burden on citizens."[9]

As late as October, Hartzler trailed Skelton, but on Election Day she triumphed. Hartzler's victory was a major achievement for the Tea Party not only because she ran against a sitting member of Congress, but also because she was one of the few women Tea Party candidates elected in 2010.[10] As such, Hartzler showed a different side of those elected as Tea Party candidates. As I demonstrated in Chapter 3, within the supporters of the Tea Party, men and women seem to hold different opinions: women more socially conservative, while men more libertarian. Hartzler's background as an advocate for socially conservative policies, such as bans on gay marriage, made her an obvious representative of Tea Party women in Congress, and also different from some of her new libertarian-leaning colleagues.

DAVID MCKINLEY

David McKinley also ran in 2010 as a Tea Party candidate, but he was not a newcomer to elected office; he had been serving in various political positions since the early 1980s. Similar to Hartzler's unconventional professional background, McKinley came to politics, not from the law, but from engineering. Prior to coming to Washington, he owned a construction firm, McKinley and Associates, based in Wheeling, West Virginia. He served in the West Virginia House of Delegates from 1981 to 1994 as well as chair of the West Virginia Republican Party. In these ways, McKinley represented another side of the Tea Party, not as an outsider or one drawn to the libertarian ideology, but as a conservative, business-oriented Republican.

In 2010, McKinley sought out the seat of Democratic congressman, Alan Mollohan, who had lost a party primary. During the campaign, McKinley spoke at the North Central West Virginia Independence Day event and signed the West Virginia Tea Party "Contract with the Citizens of West Virginia" in which he promised to promote Tea Party beliefs if elected. In return, Tea Party volunteer supporters of his candidacy conducted get-out-the-vote (GOTV) activities to get him elected.[11] In the end, with the support of the Tea Party, McKinley narrowly defeated his Democratic opponent by fewer than 1,500 votes. Once in office, McKinley tenuously balanced his background in engineering and business with his ties to the Tea Party movement.

These four new members of Congress illustrate some of the diversity of personal and professional backgrounds the Tea Party movement brought to Congress in 2011. They represented vastly different congressional districts spread across the country. They each brought different experiences and educational backgrounds to national politics. But these four, and dozens other, united under the mantle of the Tea Party, won, and then came to Washington with political power.

WHAT DID IT MEAN TO BE A TEA PARTY LEGISLATOR FROM THE CLASS OF 2010?

After the monumental election of 2010, Washington welcomed these four and a host of new members of Congress with affiliations to the Tea Party. This class of 2010 nearly all caucused with the Republicans, but many maintained their connection to the Tea Party through their affiliation with the newly formed Tea Party Caucus. Others resisted the caucus out of fears that it was too closely associated with the Republican Party and efforts to co-opt the Tea Party movement.

DEMOGRAPHICS OF TEA PARTY MEMBERS OF CONGRESS

In certain ways, the Tea Party members of Congress were well suited to represent the typical supporter of the Tea Party, since members closely reflected their average demographics. For example, unlike the youthful Justin Amash, Tea Party members of Congress were older than the average Democrat and Republican. According to analysis by Dhrumil Mehta, during the 112nd Congress (those elected in 2010, and then served from 2011 to 2012), the average age of Tea Party Republicans was 57.2 years, compared to 54.2 for non-Tea Party Republicans, and 56.6 for Democrats.[12] Tea Party members were also overwhelmingly male and, unlike Amash and Labrador, almost all white.

Tea Party members of Congress were also like many supporters of the movement because of their relative affluence. Recall from Chapter 3 that Tea Party supporters had somewhat higher median incomes than Americans in general. The same can be said for Tea Party members of Congress, but it is also true for them relative to their congressional colleagues, a group that is well known for its financial security.[13] The Center for Responsive Politics found that the net worth of the median member of the House Tea Party Caucus (a group that included not just those newly elected in 2010) was $1.8 million in 2010, including six individuals who had greater than $20 million in net worth. This compared to $755,000 for the rest of those in the House, and also more than the average non–Tea Party House Republican ($774,280) and Democrat (between $618,500 and $639,500).[14]

VOTING PATTERNS OF TEA PARTY MEMBERS OF CONGRESS

The Tea Party candidates who became Tea Party congressmen and congresswomen were then appointed to committees, and also began voting on issues upon which each had campaigned in 2010. Thus, one way to observe what it meant to be a Tea Party elected official is to examine their early legislative behavior. With hundreds of significant and insignificant votes taken each week while Congress is in session, it can be difficult to figure out where to look for comparisons of voting patterns. One option favored by political scientists is to look at outside rankings to determine voting patterns or trends. Scholars have developed some metrics, but interest groups have long scored the voting records of Congress in order to demonstrate how closely each member adheres to their particular interests. A high score from the pro-gun rights National Rifle Association (NRA), for example, suggests a member of Congress has consistently voted in the same way that the NRA would, and, conversely, a high score from the pro–gun control Brady Campaign would suggest just the opposite. A high score from the NRA is a badge of honor for those members of Congress who strongly align with those beliefs held by gun owners and gun rights believers. Right- and Left-leaning organizations now provide these "scorecards" to the public on websites.

Since 1999, one such organization, the Club for Growth, has judged member votes on fiscal issues. The Club for Growth—run for much of its history by Stephen Moore—has been an influential voice for conservative beliefs about decreasing the size of the federal government and the size of most tax policies. The organization lobbies Congress and supports candidates in support of its mission as

a national network of over 100,000 pro-growth, limited government Americans who share in the belief that prosperity and opportunity come from economic freedom. Club for Growth is the leading free-enterprise advocacy group in the nation. We win tough battles and we have an enormous influence on economic policy.[15]

As noted earlier, the Club for Growth published a study on the Tea Party class of 2010. It scored the voting decisions on tax and spending bills of 87 first-term members of the House who had campaigned as Tea Party candidates (the analysis did not examine the reelected members of the Tea Party Caucus). A score of 100% indicates a perfect allegiance with the preferences of the Club for Growth; a score of 0% indicates a perfectly contradictory voting pattern.

The mean Club for Growth score for the first-year Tea Party members was 71%. This compared to 8%, the mean score for Democrats in 2011, and 85%, the mean score for Republicans overall. The freshman class, thus, closely adhered to their Republican Party allies in Congress, but departed from the wishes of the Club for Growth. For example, Bob Dold (PA) and Patrick Meehan (PA) each received a score of 42%, and David McKinley from West Virginia, who I just described earlier, scored a 37%! Twelve Democrats scored higher than McKinley in 2011, in part because he voted against the Club for Growth position on energy subsidies, the debt limit, and several trade agreements. He also voted *against* cuts in funding for education, transportation, and agriculture. Justin Amash (MI) and Raul Labrador (ID) (as well as Tim Huelskamp (KS)), on the contrary, scored a perfect 100% because they voted with the Club position every time.

This evidence from the Club for Growth scores of the Tea Party class of 2010 suggests that there were considerable differences in general voting patterns in the first year in office compared to other groups in Congress. We can also look to these data to observe how much the Tea Party class differed from the Club for Growth preferred position on specific issues. I collected voting data from 2011 on how the new Tea Party members fared on

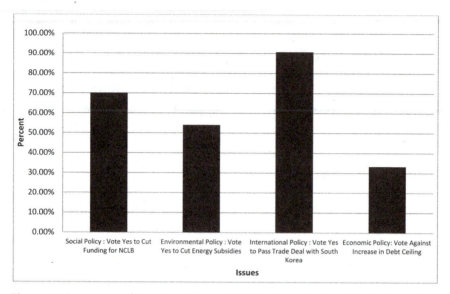

Figure 5.1 Percentage of Tea Party Class of 2010 Voting with the Club for Growth on Key Issues in 2011 (Club for Growth, Tea Party Freshman Vote Study, see http://www .clubforgrowth.org/cap-and-trade/freshmen-vote-study-just-how-tea-party-are-they/)

specific social, international, environmental, and fiscal votes. In each case, members had to decide whether to adhere to the Club for Growth recommendation or to vote otherwise. I examined four particular votes: (1) to approve cuts in energy subsidies (the Club for Growth recommended a "yes" vote); (2) to decrease funding for education contained in the No Child Left Behind (NCLB) law (the Club for Growth recommended a "yes" vote); (3) to approve a trade deal with South Korea (the Club for Growth recommended a "yes" vote); (4) to increase the federal debt limit (the Club for Growth recommended a "no" vote). I present them here, in order, from the vote with the most Tea Party consensus (trade deal) to least (debt ceiling) (see Figure 5.1).

VOTE ON TRADE DEAL

While there were considerable differences in the uniformity of voting on the four bills, there was the greatest agreement to support the trade deal with South Korea. Congress debated this bill alongside similar trade agreements with Columbia and Panama.[16] Supporters in Congress portrayed the deal with South Korea as a part of a "pro-growth" strategy to strengthen relations with a global economic powerhouse, but the bill faced opposition, mainly from Democrats in the Midwest, because of potential threats to U.S. workers. Within the Tea Party, similar lines were drawn. Recall that many were drawn to the movement because of downturns in the economy and the loss of jobs during the Great Recession of the late 2000s. For those Tea Party supporters, the pro-business, pro-market, and pro-job side of the movement was most appealing, particularly when it was framed in opposition to the president's apparent inability to create jobs and accusations of his socialist proclivities. But for others, particularly Tea Party members in the Midwest, job losses were also tied to a narrative about unfair foreign competition and globalization. For these Tea Party supporters, the economic protectionist and isolationist traditions of U.S. history drew them to the movement. Thus, this vote on the trade agreement with South Korea played to two competing impulses in the Tea Party movement, and Tea Party legislators likely faced very different levels of constituent sentiment, based on the location and characteristics of their district.

In the final October vote, which the Club for Growth supported, the bill passed with a large majority in the House (278–151) and in the Senate (83–15). Overall, more than 90% of the Tea Party class of 2010 voted "yes," leaving just a handful voting "no." Eight of the 21 Republican "no" votes were from the Tea Party class of 2010. Justin Amash, Vicki Jo Hartzler, and Raul Labrador all voted for the bill, but David McKinley broke with his Tea Party colleagues and from the wishes of the Club for Growth and voted "no." In explaining his vote, McKinley pointed to his constituents in West Virginia:

As a proud West Virginian who grew up in an era when steelworkers in the Northern Panhandle numbered some 30,000, I cannot support the kind of agreements that helped cause that figure to dwindle to 2,000 today. Because these trade agreements may harm northern West Virginia, I remain committed to working with my colleagues in Congress on developing a long-term manufacturing policy in this country that helps stop the hemorrhaging of our jobs overseas and strengthens our middle class.[17]

He explained that two local business owners, Beri Fox, whose company produced marbles in Paden City, West Virginia, and another, Joe Wells III, whose company made china in Newell, West Virginia, had written to him to express their wishes that he vote "no." Rather than adhering to the recommendations of the Club for Growth and to the direction of many others in the Tea Party, McKinley, perhaps deferring to his own history in business, decided that the local dimensions of the trade bill were not right for his district. But McKinley was the clear outlier, as most in the Tea Party voted together and aligned with the Club for Growth.

VOTE ON EDUCATION FUNDING

There was somewhat less agreement within the Tea Party class of 2010 on reducing funding for education. As noted earlier, among Tea Party supporters there was deep concern for federal spending, but also for the existence of the federal Department of Education. Opposition to federal involvement in education policy has long been a tenet of conservative, states-rights advocates, and certain Republican leaders for decades—perhaps most famously President Ronald Reagan—have called for the end of the agency's existence.[18] Despite the popularity of antifederal government calls to close the Education Department, cutting funding for local public schools comes with a different set of risks for members of Congress with constituents who have children in public schools and others who are employed in the school system. Even if Tea Party supporters chafed at the federal source of the funds, the money from NCLB ultimately trickles down to schools in their own communities. Much like the trade vote, the education funding vote did not neatly align with any single Tea Party value.

Tea Party members faced this dilemma during a 2011 vote on funding for certain literacy programs within NCLB, the federal law that funds various aspects of kindergarten to grade 12 education.[19] When the final vote was held, 70% of the Tea Party class voted "yes." The vote, which temporarily sealed $750 million in cuts to programs such as Striving Readers, Reading Is Fundamental, and Teach for America, also earned a sharp rebuke from no less than actor, Matt Damon, who called the Tea Party "completely intransigent."[20]

But to overgeneralize about the Tea Party's role in this vote would be wrong. Around a third (30%) of the Tea Party freshman voted "no," in opposition to the wishes of the Club for Growth and contrary to Damon's assertion. Justin Amash voted "yes" in favor of the cuts, as did the former educator, Vicky Jo Hartzler. But, as with the trade deal vote, David McKinley again deviated from his Tea Party colleagues and voted "no" in opposition to the cuts. And, interestingly, Raul Labrador also voted "no," diverging from many in the Tea Party and also, for one of the few times, from the Club for Growth.

VOTE ON ENERGY BILL

There was even less agreement within the Tea Party on energy subsidies. For some supporters of the Tea Party, energy subsidies were a part of a regime of unnecessary corporate welfare that had to end. For those opposed to subsidies, they often claimed that the free and open market should determine the future of energy, farm, and transportation industries, not the federal government. Writing in the *Washington Times*, Raul Labrador and Congressman Mike Pompeo concluded: "[The bill] would eliminate all energy tax credits, each of which is nothing more than a taxpayer handout to politically favored industries or companies. From solar to wind, from geothermal to biomass and from ethanol to hydrogen, they all must go."[21] The vote to cut $3 billion of spending on the Energy Department—an amendment to an Energy and Water appropriations bill (H.R. 2354)—tested this belief, because there were equally loud voices from other wings of the conservative movement, especially representatives of U.S. energy companies, which approved of tax incentives as a way to make American businesses competitive with foreign companies.[22] Moreover, cutting subsidies given to energy companies could also cost U.S. jobs, another major priority for Tea Party supporters. Since energy subsidies often go to companies based in states with large numbers of Tea Party supporters, including those across the Midwest and West, this was a complex issue for certain Tea Party members of Congress.

But a vote on energy subsidies also has deep implications for the environment. Tea Party supporters are some of the most skeptical and least concerned about global warming. Research by Anthony Leiserowitz et al. found that a majority (51%) of Tea Party supporters were "not at all worried" about global warming (compared to 29% of Republicans and only 8% of Democrats) and the same majority (51%) thought that global warming will "never" harm people in the United States (compared to 33% of Republicans and 7% of Democrats).[23] The study also found that Tea Party supporters were the least likely to support new taxes to pay for increased home energy efficiency (52% of Tea Party supporters "strong oppose" compared to the 35% of Republicans and 17% of Democrats). Tea Party members of Congress faced these very different environmental attitudes of their constituents.

In the end, Tea Party members were evenly split on the vote to cut energy subsidies: 54% voted "yes" and 46% voted "no." Labrador and Amash both voted "yes" in support of the subsidy cuts, while McKinley and Hartzler both voted "no" in opposition to the subsidy cuts. And the even split between these four mirrored the overall mixed congressional view of the cuts. The proposed amendment ultimately failed in the House because fewer than 100 Republicans voted in support, half from the Tea Party class of 2010.

VOTE TO INCREASE THE DEBT LIMIT

The greatest departure from the wishes of the Club for Growth came on one of the most controversial issues of the legislative session: the vote to increase the federal debt limit. This issue, which drew heated media coverage, has historically been viewed as merely a procedural decision that typically passes in Congress with nearly 100% agreement. Increasing the debt limit confirms that the U.S. government will in fact pay off the debts it has already accrued in the past. But, the regularity of the increases, and massive size of the national debt, aligned with other powerful symbols for the Tea Party. Many in the Tea Party movement came to view this issue as synonymous with all that was wrong with Washington and, at least symbolic way, as a way to voice their discontent with the size of federal spending.

On August 2, the federal government would hit the debt ceiling, necessitating the need for a congressional vote authorizing another increase. The implications of a "no" vote were murky, but in the worst-case scenario, experts argued that if the federal government was unable to repay debts already accrued, global financial markets would react badly and the international community would lose faith in their U.S. investments.

Tea Party activists saw the vote as a critical moment for Congress. One of the leading activists, William Temple, chair of the National Tea Party Convention, dressed in full colonial attire, argued: "We will be judging the House Republicans and their Democratic colleagues on one issue only: Did you vote for more debt? That's it. . . . Red ink requires pink slips, federal layoffs and downsizing for D.C.'s ruling class just like the rest of us out there."[24] Temple reflected the purity of the debt ceiling issue for the Tea Party: it was a litmus test for members of Congress used to show whether they were truly with the movement or simply willing to compromise on core principles.

And some members of Congress concurred. Raul Labrador told PBS:

In the past, the debt ceiling had just been a simple vote that was done, and people raised the debt ceiling. There were a few negotiations. But when you're only one-half of one-third of the government, you have to look for those moments where you can actually have leverage over the negotiations. And the debt ceiling was something that had to be done; it had to be raised if government was going to continue being effective and working. So this was a moment where we could all actually get something out of the deal. The issue was that many of the freshmen . . . had made a pledge that they were not going to raise the debt ceiling under any circumstances. And I think leadership was also worried about that pledge that they had made, because then if they wouldn't even look at any circumstance where they were willing to raise the debt ceiling, then we were going to have an impasse here in Washington, DC.[25]

The pledge that Labrador described could potentially tie the hands of Tea Party freshman if a debt increase was contained in a bill with other preferred cuts and reforms. Negotiation was seen as a sign of political weakness and departure from the purity of the Tea Party beliefs. But as the summer progressed, Tea Party members indicated some willingness to negotiate. Justin Amash released a statement that read: "As I have said consistently since before I was a Representative in Congress, I will not consider voting to raise the federal government's debt ceiling unless the vote is tied to fundamental reform such as a repeal of the President's onerous healthcare legislation or passage of a well-structured balanced budget amendment to the Constitution."[26] And David McKinley wrote an op-ed in his local paper that argued: "I refuse to give this fiscally reckless president my vote to raise the debt ceiling unless he agrees to pair it with major structural restraints on Congress' ability to spend money."[27]

On July 31, members of Congress and President Obama reached an agreement on raising the debt limit in exchange for several measures to reduce federal spending upward of $2 trillion, the establishment of a joint selection committee that would quickly address debt reduction, and limits on new revenue collection. On August 1, the House passed the bill 269–174, with 66 Republicans voting against the deal, 29 of whom were a part of the Tea Party class of 2010. Hartzler, Amash, and Labrador all voted against "no," but McKinley, again the renegade, voted "yes" with the majority that passed the debt increase and the majority (66%) of the Tea party class of 2010.

Out of these four votes, a more complex image of Tea Party legislators emerges. On one side, we have Tea Party stalwarts, Amash and Labrador. They consistently voted with the majority of the Tea Party class of 2010, but also in line with the Club for Growth. For this reason, each scored a perfect 100% from that group, and became Tea Party darlings and emerging national leaders. Hartzler also generally stuck with her Tea Party brethren, but was less in line with the Club for Growth. She scored a 70% from the Club for Growth, which made her quite similar to the rest of the class of 2010. Recall that the mean score from the Club for Growth for members of the class of 2010 was 71%. David McKinley, though, was the real outlier among the class of 2010. Not only did he depart from his colleagues on many of votes described earlier on education, trade, debt, and energy, but he also scored only a 37% from the Club for Growth during his first year in Congress.

In Chapter 3, I showed certain differences in the political views of Tea Party supporters in different parts of the country. It is worth considering whether these differences were reflected in the voting patterns of members of Congress. At least in theory, members are supposed to reflect the local concerns and beliefs of constituents, and since these seemed to vary from region to region for the Tea Party, then maybe Tea Party members of Congress from southern states might be voting differently than those from other parts of the country. To examine this, I compared the 40 members of the class of 2010 that represented southern states to the 47 representing other parts of the country. In three of the four votes described earlier, there were statistically significant differences in voting patterns. On the vote to defund NCLB, those from outside of the South were evenly split (23 "no" and 24 "yes"), while in South there was near consensus (3 "no" and 37 "yes"), a statistically significant difference (using the Chi^2 test and a p-value $< .01$). Those in the South were more likely to vote against the trade bill (7 "no" and 33 "yes") compared to outside of the South where almost all voted in favor (just 1 "no"), also a statistically significant difference (at the p-value $< .05$ level). On the important debt ceiling vote, members in the South were evenly split (17 "no" and 23 "yes") versus a large majority outside of the South (12 "no" and 35 "yes"), a statistically significant difference (at the p-value $< .10$ level). Only on the vote on cutting energy subsidies was geography not clearly related to voting. Tea Party representatives in the House from the South were evenly split (57% voted "yes") as were those outside the South (52% "yes"), not a statistically significant difference. What this suggests is that the regionalism that showed up in public opinion within the Tea Party was reflected in voting behavior in Congress. Southern Tea Party members of Congress voted in significantly different ways than those outside the South, and more in line with the wishes of the Club for Growth.

With these regional differences noted, could those voting against the Club for Growth survive? Could McKinley, in particular, continue to be a Tea Party maverick and persist with his pattern of voting outside of the Tea Party norms? Or might others in the Tea Party, Tea Party activists in his district, and even the Club for Growth change his mind and discipline his intransigence? If we look beyond the first year of legislative behavior, we can see Congressman McKinley's voting patterns slowly align much more closely with others in the Tea Party and the Club for Growth. Over time, Congressman McKinley increased his Club score to 57% in 2012 and 60% in 2013. And rather than lose his reelection bid in 2012, he succeeded and remained in Congress. It is not clear what drove him toward the voting profile of the typical Tea Party member of Congress, but this change in his voting patterns, as much of the rest of this book has demonstrated, was much more dynamic and varied than most conventional accounts suggest.

And McKinley was not alone in changing his voting patterns. According to the Club for Growth, Justin Amash became somewhat less consistent, his rating dropped from 100% to 99% in 2013. Labrador dropped even further, from 100% down to 86% in 2013. In fact, among those Tea Party members in the class of 2010 that were most alike the Club for Growth, none went up, and only Trey Gowdy and Jeff Duncan (both from SC) maintained the same score of 97%. Two, Joe Walsh (IL) and Ben Quayle (AZ), lost the reelection in 2012 and couldn't be scored again. Similarly, at the bottom end of the scale, only Steve Stivers (OH), Joe Heck (NV), and Steve Womack (AR) saw their Club for Growth scores go up—20 percentage points for Heck—the remainder all scored lower in 2013 than they initially had in 2011.

There are many reasons for these changes in Tea Party member voting patterns, but one compelling general explanation relates to the declining approval of the Tea Party that I described in Chapter 3. We know from previous research that, prior to the 2010 election, the size of Tea Party protests in a district increased how conservatively members of Congress voted.[28] But we also know that the focus on protesting waned for the Tea Party in the second phase of the movement, and overall support for the Tea Party decreased as well in many districts. The Pew Research Center for the People and the Press compared the favorability of the Tea Party when the class of 2010 was elected, November 2010, to one year after, November 2011.[29] They then compared the attitudes of the general public and the attitudes of those living in Tea Party districts. One would expect that the Tea Party might lose support in districts that had not previously elected a Tea Party member of Congress. And this is what happened: agreement with the Tea Party dropped from approximately 27% to around 20%, and disagreement rose from just under 26% to 27%. What is more interesting is that the same pattern occurred to a greater extent in districts that had just one year earlier elected a Tea Party candidate. At the time of the 2010 election, in Tea Party districts, around 33% of the public agreed with the Tea Party and less than 20% disagreed. This is one of the reasons why Tea Party candidates could win. But just one year later, support dropped to 25%, and disagreement had risen to 23%. What this suggests is that Tea Party districts came to more closely resemble non–Tea Party districts, and Tea Party members of Congress now represented fewer and fewer constituents who aligned closely with the movement. This does not explain the change in David McKinley's movement in the more conservative direction, but it does explain why many other Tea Party members changed their voting patterns and saw their Club for Growth score go down.

There are other explanations for these changes in voting, but what this shows is that rather than voting as a unified group on every vote, Tea Party members diverged on certain policy issues and varied in subsequent years. The range in agreement across the four votes described earlier shows that the Tea Party movement represented in Congress was just as varied as the Tea Party organizations and Tea Party supporters. Members balanced their allegiance to the movement with other concerns for non–Tea Party constituents, the Republican Party, and their own values. This variation runs somewhat counter to what some researchers have concluded about the Tea Party. For example, Chris Parker, author of some of the seminal work on the Tea Party, was interviewed about his research on the movement. When asked why the Tea Party was so effective, he said: "Because they won't compromise. You've got about 52 members of the Republican conference who are affiliated with the tea party in some official way. That's a bit less than a quarter of all House Republicans. That's enough in the House. They refuse to compromise because, to them, compromise is capitulation."[30] Parker may have been right, in general, but when we look at the actual voting on specific bills, there was a lot more diversity of opinion across the Tea Party than we would expect from a group that always refused to compromise.

HOW DID THE TEA PARTY ENDORSE CANDIDATES DURING THE 2012 CAMPAIGN?

At the start of the book, I argued that the second phase of the Tea Party began with the November 2010 congressional election, the legislative decisions of Tea Party elected officials, and the shift from political outsiders to political insiders. I also argued in Chapter 2 that the second phase of the Tea Party movement saw the organizations of the Tea Party, particularly those national organizations, growing increasingly professionalized, sophisticated, and oriented toward politics and elections. For this reason, the congressional election of 2012 is also worth investigating. The changing emphasis of Tea Party organizations meant that they increasingly viewed elections as a major part of their political strategy, and would use congressional votes taken in 2012 as a basis to fire up supporters. Following the vote on the debt ceiling, Tea Party activist William Temple said to the *Wall Street Journal*: "I was looking for something to get the tea party active. . . . I've already got all sorts of tea-party people emailing me saying, 'Let's get on the buses.'"[31] But as with other aspects of the Tea Party movement, national organizations varied in terms of how they approached 2012, which candidates they supported, and ultimately, how successful those candidates were in the 2012 election.

To investigate this, I rely again on the excellent research of the Institute for Research and Education on Human Rights (IREHR). Researchers collected information on how the political action committees (PACs) of three of the national organizations (TPE, FreedomWorks, and Patriot Action Network) endorsed candidates (Tea Party Patriots (TPP) did not make endorsements). This research shows some degree of agreement in Senate and House races, but many differences. For example, all three groups endorsed Josh Mandel in the Ohio Senate race. Mandel eventually lost.

All three endorsed Ted Cruz for the Senate in Texas, and he won. But in the remaining Senate races where at least one of the three made an endorsement, there was no consensus. FreedomWorks and TPPE endorsed Richard Mourdock (IN), John Raese (WV), and Tom Smith (PA), but the Patriot Action Network did not. FreedomWorks alone endorsed seven other Senate candidates, but only one, Jeff Flake (AZ), won.

In the House, the situation was even more varied and more successful. In 2012, Tea Party organizations made endorsements in 84 congressional races and the candidate won 80% of the time (or 67 races).[32] The degree of agreement in the House races was even less pronounced than in the Senate, in part due to the fact that the Patriot Action Network made so few endorsements. By far, the Patriot Action Network made the smallest number endorsements of the three, endorsing only Mia Love (who lost in UT), Justin Amash (who won reelection in MI), and Dan Benishek (who also won reelection in MI). FreedomWorks made endorsements in all but eight races, and backed the losing candidate in only 10. The most interesting may be the TPE. It endorsed 14 candidates, but lost in half of those races. TPE backed the losing candidates in Florida (twice), Illinois, Georgia, Pennsylvania, Arizona, and North Carolina.

Given the organizational histories I presented in Chapter 2 of the book, these differences in electoral tactics and relative success should not come as a surprise. FreedomWorks operated long before 2009, had an established political infrastructure, and had a leadership team with considerable experience with electoral politics. We know that FreedomWorks was less prominent in the first phase of the Tea Party, when most of the activity was on the grassroots level and focused on mobilizing supporters for outsider tactics such as protesting. But as the movement shifted to the second phase and became more centered in Washington, the tactical strengths of FreedomWorks emerged. The success FreedomWorks had in endorsing winning candidates is one demonstration of how important the organization was to the second phase of the movement.

TPE, on the other hand, was established in 2009, at the start of the first phase. TPE was solely focused on electoral politics, and the organization was structured to support candidates and not help organize local chapters or protest marches. The second phase might have been a boon for TPE, since it was dominated by elections. Yet, TPE had much less success than one might expect. During this second phase of the movement, TPE was unable to use its focused expertise to back many congressional winners. Of course, each campaign is different, and organizations sometimes back candidates they know are going to lose in the general election. One of the primary strategies of some in the Tea Party has been to challenge established Republicans in the primaries, knowing that a general election victory would be difficult. In the cases, a failed endorsement might actually be a success.

Finally, Patriot Action Network showed only limited interest in using the electoral tactic of endorsing candidates. They backed only two winners, and both were congressional incumbents. Patriot Action Network remained focused on other tactics during the second phase, as the other large national organization, TPP, did as well.

CONCLUSION

The second phase of the Tea Party movement saw a shift in political tactics, political actors, and geography. The center of the Tea Party moved from local cities and towns to Washington, D.C. Organizations and activists stopped registering new domain names and slowed their coordination of protests, and began to form political action committees, distribute campaign donations, and endorse candidates. And, as a result, newly elected members of Congress now could legitimately speak on behalf of the Tea Party, having been elected as Tea Party candidates in 2010. These are great changes in how to understand the Tea Party movement from the first phase, and these were changes that were not always smooth. The Roanoke Tea Party was caught in this shift, pushed out of the federation it helped to form because of the increasingly complicated internal politics of campaigns and elections. Change isn't easy.

Many have focused on this phase as one defined by Tea Party members' refusal to negotiate and compromise. The Tea Party class of 2010 and Tea Party Caucus have been portrayed as so fiercely committed to ideological purity and pledges of fealty to the cause, that they were willing to harm the nation and the common good.[33] There is a line of truth to this explanation of the second phase of the Tea Party, but there is also evidence of variation and disagreement. Tea Party candidates varied in how they were elected, some products of the same political traditions that have defined the country for two hundred years, while others who brought new perspectives and backgrounds to Washington. While the typical Tea Party member of Congress resembled the typical Tea Party supporter, some of the most notable leaders in Washington were quite different.

Once in Washington, the voting patterns of Tea Party members varied to a greater extent than conventional explanations acknowledge. On the four bills studied in this chapter, Tea Party members varied from near-unanimity to great disagreement. They also varied notably in how aligned they were with other conservative organizations, such that some members, like Congressman David McKinley, were barely recognizable as Tea Party crusaders. Some of these differences can be explained by geography. We learned from this chapter that southern Tea Party members of Congress voted in significantly different ways than those outside the South, perhaps a reflection of how attuned each group was to the wishes of their constituents.

As the Tea Party moved toward the 2012 election, we see further evidence of variation. The major national Tea Party organizations pursued quite different electoral strategies, and with varying levels of success. FreedomWorks had an effective and robust plan to endorse and support candidates, while others mustered only a limited and largely ineffective electoral strategy. Given the organizational backgrounds of these groups, this should come as no surprise.

Thus, from this chapter I hope to have complemented what has already been presented on the organizations, people, and supporters of the Tea Party. The Tea Party legislators drew on the range of sources of support (financial, organizational, and electoral) that helped them land in Washington. Once in Washington, each sought to advance the interest of the Tea Party in different ways. Whether these members continue to behave in these ways or find a new legislative strategy will largely determine the future of the Tea Party. The next chapter speculates as to what that future might look like. The chapter explores a number of possible directions for Tea Party futures.

Chapter 6

Anticipating Tea Party Futures

The aim of this book has been to grapple with two aspects of the Tea Party: (1) the diversity that exists within the movement and (2) the changes associated with the shift from the first to the second phase of the movement. When we look closely at the people, the organizations, and the supporters of the Tea Party, there is much more variety than common explanations have acknowledged. The substantial numbers of Tea Party libertarians, Tea Party Democrats, and Tea Party women alter the conventional notions of what a Tea Party supporter looks like and believes. The organizations also vary greatly, from the most local grassroots organization with a few dozen dedicated members and a budget of almost nothing to multimillion-dollar professional lobbying operations based in Washington. Diversity is as much a defining characteristic of the Tea party as is the belief in personal liberty or opposition to President Obama.

There were also notable shifts in the tone and mechanics of the movement from the first phase (February 2009 to November 2010) to the second (December 2010 onward). The movement shifted or matured from mainly outsider and protest-oriented tactics to insider tactics focused on elections. The first phase was dominated by organizing and mobilizing, while the second phase was focused on campaigning and lobbying. Media coverage shifted from Fox News Network's near-monopoly to a broader array of coverage, including prominent and often critical coverage by MSNBC.

A number of vexing questions remain about the Tea Party, perhaps most prominently a question about phases: If it has not already, when will the third phase begin? I argued at the start of the book that the first phase of the Tea Party movement began in February 2009. I also showed how even this starting point is somewhat artificial, since much of the foundation of the Tea Party rested on decades of intellectual work supported by many of the same funders who supported the movement after 2009. But for the sake of measurement, what existed prior to February 2009 was almost never called a Tea Party and most activists and supporters point to that month and Rick Santelli's CNBC rant as the starting point. What happened after February also attests to this being the start of the first phase, since in the following weeks and months there was nearly unprecedented organizing and mobilizing. Hundreds of groups formed in advance of Tax Day 2009 and hundreds more continued to form as Independence Day approached.

That first phase, therefore, was characterized by the work of organizing. Like they did in Roanoke, Virginia, activists met to discuss organizational rules, procedures, and mission. They created websites, began tweeting and posting on Facebook, and communicated with potential supporters. They sought permits from city government, created banners, and decided who would speak to hundreds and thousands gathered at rallies.

All of this was done under an umbrella of beliefs in smaller government, personal liberty, and tax cuts. Anger—particularly directed at President Obama, but also at undocumented immigrants and those who received government aid—energized activists and supporters of the movement. The venom of the first phase of the Tea Party cannot be ignored, as it demarcates Tea Party supporters from non–Tea Party Republicans, and even some Tea Party libertarians, who largely shared on ideology and agreed on many policy proposals, but who were not motivated by the same level of outrage. Furthermore, most Tea Party activists could not be called racist, but the tone and tenor of their anger and rhetoric could not be detached from long traditions of racial politics in the United States. Even if they occurred only occasionally, the racist, homophobic, and anti-immigrant messages at certain Tea Party rallies and posted on Tea Party websites defined the movement in the eyes of much of the public.

The Tea Party was a decentralized outsider movement of protesters and activists until November 2010. I argue in the book that the congressional election, which saw dozens of new members of Congress elected with strong ties to the Tea Party, represents the end of the first phase and the start of the second. Tea Party members of Congress shared many of the views of Tea Party supporters of the first phase, and much of the anger, but they now had the power to legislate. The second phase was then much more centralized in Washington and dominated by policymaking. Tea Party members of Congress were not nearly as homogeneous as news accounts suggest, but they can be credited (or blamed) for many of the important legislative events during their first term in Washington. The intractable debt ceiling debates of 2011 demonstrated the vitality of a group of legislators with only weak ties to the Republican Party and the party's powerful lobbying allies.

As such, the more traditional wing of the Republican Party began to push back during the second phase of the movement. Established interest groups, such as those that represent key U.S. industries, increasingly supported non-Tea Party Republicans, and some of the most important backers of the Tea Party, including the organizations associated with the Koch brothers, shifted to opposing the president, rather than Democratic members of the House. Americans for Prosperity (AFP), for example, decreased campaign spending from $33.5 million in 2012 to just $4.4 million in 2014, while the U.S. Chamber of Commerce spent $35.4 million in 2014 to back what were deemed non–Tea Party Republican candidates in North Carolina, Iowa, and Colorado. Much of the energy and enthusiasm for the Tea Party, both broadly within the American public and within political elites in Washington, waned during the second phase. Media outlets, such as MSNBC, shared in this turn, providing a much more critical reading of the movement than we saw in the first phase. And the moderate side of the party, not the Tea Party, was ultimately credited with winning back control of the Senate from the Democrats in the 2014 election.

But at the end of 2014, the Tea Party also changed. Tea Party organizations, which had been the champion of failed challengers and outsiders in previous elections, endorsed 30 incumbents in the House who won.[1] Merely 18 of the Tea Party-endorsed candidates in the House who won in 2014 were challenging sitting members of Congress. The trend in the Senate was a little less pronounced, but the success rate was even stronger: 80% of Tea Party-endorsed Senate candidates won, of whom nine were challengers. As the Republican Party pushed back, the Tea Party responded, grew more institutionalized, and was much more politically successful in the end. The end of the second phase for the Tea Party, then, demonstrated a degree of political and strategic maturation that the larger conversation about moderate Republican influence overlooked.

So, what now? What will happen to the future of the Tea Party? With the completion of the 2014 midterm election that saw a few Tea Party challengers sent home early, but many other Tea Party candidates win for the second time, has the second phase of the Tea Party ended and a more mature third phase commenced? And if so, what are the potential directions the Tea Party movement might take in this third phase with Republican control of Congress? If the first phase was defined by organizing and the second by legislating, what will define the third? Continued maturation or extinction? I argue throughout the rest of the chapter that there are a number of potential directions for the Tea Party, and that the midterm elections in 2014 marked the end of the second phase and the start of the third phase. This third phase, I contend, will likely be dominated by the long political campaign in advance of the 2016 presidential election. There are a number of reasons for this. First, presidential campaigns have grown longer and more expensive. In 2008, Senator John McCain spent $333 million and President Obama spent $730 million.[2] In 2012, President Obama and Governor Romney each spent about a billion dollars. If the trend of attention to the presidential campaign continues along its current trajectory, total spending will easily top $4 billion, the estimate for the midterm campaigns in 2014. The large amount of spending demonstrated in Chapter 4 will likely be drawn into this presidential campaign. Second, the natural evolution of the Tea Party from outsider to congressional insiders will continue along this path with a broad focus on the presidential race. In the second phase, this focus was on opposing President Obama, in part because there was no Tea Party opposition candidate. In 2016, this is likely to change, as at least three prominent Tea Party Republican candidates appear ready for legitimate challenges. Senator Rand Paul, Senator Marco Rubio, and former Alaska governor Sarah Palin each have strong connections to various wings of the Tea Party and each is in a position to run a competitive campaign.

Another trajectory for the Tea Party could run in the opposite direction. Rather than elevating up the ladder of U.S. politics, as a focus on the presidential race would suggest, another path could be toward broadening the Tea Party message on new issues. The second phase of the Tea Party saw alignment in Washington behind primarily conservative Republican members of Congress and issues about health, tax, and budget policy, but we know that there are Tea Party supporters with other ideological backgrounds and different interests. Around certain issues, the Tea Party could foster a broad-based coalition of unlikely allies. In particular, issues such as international trade, medical marijuana, and education reform might offer a way to find new friends and broaden the Tea Party movement in the third phase. This is also a possibility because of the growing frustration of local Tea Party activists. Many grew disenchanted by shifts that occurred in the second phase of the movement. As such, a broadened Tea Party message might also be associated with a more localized movement and return to the roots of the movement in February 2009.

To be clear, making predictions about the future is always dicey. I collected the data presented in this chapter primarily from polling conducted in 2013 and 2014. Polls vary greatly in the years leading up to a presidential race—recall that for a time in 2011 Herman Cain was seen as the front-runner for the Republican presidential nomination—so the arguments made here should be read with that in mind. Emboldened by Republican control of the House and Senate, other issues and candidates may emerge in 2015 and 2016 that will greatly alter the future of the Tea Party. I present several possibilities based on what is known up through 2014, at the tail end of the second phase of the Tea Party movement, fully acknowledging the chances that the predictions will need to be revised as political circumstances change.

INVESTING IN THE PRESIDENTIAL RACE

As I noted earlier, spending on presidential campaigns has grown considerably over the last three election cycles. Money spent directly by candidates has grown, but money spent by outside organizations has also ballooned. As I argued in Chapter 4, the *Citizens United* decision is commonly blamed for this, but this trend began long before the decision was issued in 2010. The second phase of the Tea Party, in fact, was defined by this spending. Tea Party supporters contributed to candidates, but also bought millions of dollars of independent political advertisements to oppose the president and certain policies, especially the Affordable Care Act (ACA), also known as Obamacare. But in 2012, there was no prominent Tea Party candidate running for the presidency. Governor Mitt Romney likely won the votes of many Tea Party supporters, but most Tea Party activists remained lukewarm on supporting him directly, as he embodied many of the attributes of moderate Republican candidates of the past, including Senator Robert Dole and Senator John McCain. In looking ahead to 2016, this is likely to change. While there are numerous possible candidates, there are at least three prominent individuals who offer the possibility that a Tea Party favorite will be in the running for the White House: Senator Marco Rubio (FL), Senator Rand Paul (KY), and Governor Sarah Palin (AK). Each represents a dimension of the Tea Party, each has had strong support among Tea Party activists, and each has expressed an interest in the office. I explore the possibility of each without offering predictions as to the likelihood of them winning the presidential race, rather to expose and illustrate future dimensions and directions of the Tea Party.

SENATOR MARCO RUBIO

Many recent presidential contests have been fought in the state of Florida. The closely divided and large electorate has meant that the sunshine state is also a classic swing state. So closely politically divided that it took the Supreme Court to divvy up the state's electoral college votes in 2000 and award the White House to President George W. Bush. Winning the presidency has recently come down to courting Florida's support: President Bush narrowly won the state in 2000 and again in 2004; President Obama won by a similarly tight margin in 2008 and 2012.

Florida also provided the Tea Party with one of the movement's first notable electoral victories. In 2010, State House of Representatives member, Marco Rubio, defeated the state's former Republican governor, Charlie Crist, to win the Republican Senate nomination. Crist was broadly popular in the state at the time, but a moderate, who later ran as an Independent and then as a Democrat for governor. The Tea Party targeted Crist for his policy positions and routinely mocked his tarmac embrace of President Obama in 2009.[3] Rubio was a popular option for the Tea Party supporters, and he went on to defeat Crist and the Democrat, Kendrick Meeks, in the general election, marking a major success for the Tea Party's ability to challenge both moderate Republicans and defeat Democrats.

On the day after his 2010 victory, the *Washington Post* headline read: "Marco Rubio, from Exile to Tea Party Hero."[4] Rubio is the son of Cuban immigrants, and thus diverges from the common portrait of a Tea Party leader. The newspaper quoted the leader of the Central Florida Tea Party: "[Rubio] understands the plight of the common man a lot better than most because of his background. . . . That really resonates with tea party folks." He drew support from his heritage, his youth, and his conservative stance on key policy issues. In particular, he was lauded for his positions on tax and spending bills that are important to the Tea Party (he was given a 97% score from the Club for Growth in 2011) as well as his focus on "American exceptionalism."[5] He also was viewed as a social conservative on issues such as abortion and gay marriage, earning perfect 100% scores from the National Right to Life Committee, the Family Research Council, and the Catholic Advocate.[6]

The Tea Party helped Rubio get elected in 2010, and they remained committed to him during the 2012 election. During the run-up to the 2012 Republican convention in Florida, it was Rubio whom many in the Tea Party wanted chosen to be Mitt Romney's running mate. The Tea Party Express (TPE) published results of an internal poll that found two-thirds of those they polled ranked Rubio as the strongest candidate, followed by the eventual choice, Congressman Paul Ryan (WI), who was supported as a strong candidate by 50% of those polled.[7]

But Marco Rubio's future as a favorite among Tea Party activists began to dwindle as soon as he pursued comprehensive immigration reform. In April 2013, Rubio introduced a bill in the Senate, the "Border Security,

Economic Opportunity & Immigration Modernization Act of 2013," along with seven Senate colleagues ("The Gang of 8") including Republican senators John McCain (AZ) and Lindsay Graham (SC) and Democrats Chuck Schumer (NY) and Dick Durbin (IL). In defending the merits of the bill, Rubio wrote:

Our immigration system is broken, and the status quo of having 11 million undocumented people living under de facto amnesty will only continue if we do nothing to solve this problem. This bill marks the beginning of an important debate, and I believe it will fix our broken system by securing our borders, improving interior enforcement, modernizing our legal immigration to help create jobs and protect American workers, and dealing with our undocumented population in a tough but humane way that is fair to those trying to come here the right way and linked to achieving several security triggers.[8]

The bipartisan bill addressed many of the important and widely debated issues including the introduction of an e-verify system for companies to electronically check the work status of employees, a guest worker program, and changes in high-skilled immigration procedures. But it was the "tough but humane way" of treating undocumented population that drew fire from the Tea Party. As demonstrated in Chapter 3, immigration has been one of the policy issues that Tea Party supporters, particularly in certain parts of the country, were most enflamed by. As I showed earlier, some Tea Party organizations even formed common cause with anti-immigrant groups like the Minutemen to oppose immigration from Mexico and laws that made the children of undocumented residents eligible for certain public programs.

Rubio's bill would have given temporary legal status to those without documentation after certain border security changes had been made and the outcomes measured. Even though this approach to the large number of undocumented residents living in the country was a compromise from what most Democrats and immigration advocates preferred, the Tea Party protested vigorously. The *Washington Post* reported on a June 2013 rally in Washington by the Tea Party. Instead of lauding Senator Rubio as a movement champion, Dana Milbank reported that activists held signs that read: "'Rubio RINO' (Republican in Name Only) and 'Rubio Lies, Americans Die.'"[9] The crowd called for someone to "Primary Rubio!" as he had just three years earlier to Charlie Crist.

The damage done to Marco Rubio's future as a Tea Party darling greatly diminished his potential run for the presidency, though, Quinnipiac University reported on a poll that showed Rubio's support in Florida did not go down at quite the rate we might have expected.[10] From February 2010 to June 2013, Rubio's favorability ranking remained between 44% and 41% in general. But further from home and among Tea Party supporters, Senator Rubio's hopes for a Tea Party–backed run for the presidency dwindled at the start of the third phase of the movement.

The great irony of Senator Rubio's loss of support from the base of the Tea Party during the second phase of the movement is that he provided so many assets for a run for national office. For the Tea Party to back a winning candidate, that person likely needs to be able to broaden the support from the movement's core constituents. The minority of nonconservative Tea Party supporters mentioned in Chapter 3, including Independents and Democrats, could be drawn to the bipartisan efforts to address immigration. As important, the growing size of the Hispanic American population, for whom immigration is a salient political issue, also might be attracted to a candidate who has worked on addressing the complexity of immigration issues. A candidate who could also descriptively represent Hispanic American voters would also certainly be an asset for the chances of the Tea Party to back a winner. No Hispanic American candidate has been chosen to represent the Republican or Democratic Party on a national ticket, meaning Marco Rubio would be carving new ground for a major voting bloc.

But the uncompromising tendencies of the Tea Party—tendencies that verge on an ethos—make a Tea Party-backed run for Senator Marco Rubio less and less likely, even as his support among mainstream Republicans may grow. He rose on the brash intraparty politics of challenging mainstream Republican, and could suffer from the same fate in 2016. For Tea Party supporters to back Rubio for president, they would need to forgive him for what has been framed as a major offense: compromising with the enemy and reneging on a campaign promise.

GOVERNOR SARAH PALIN

Another favorite of the Tea Party has been Sarah Palin, the former governor of Alaska and Republican vice presidential candidate in 2008. To consider Governor Palin a contender for the presidency in 2016 is either laughable or exceedingly obvious, depending on how you view her political accomplishments. Many still mock her portrayals on television and well-known gaffes in nationally broadcast interviews. She appeared with her family in a reality television show and often seems more interested in her television career as a political pundit on Fox News, than in governing. She even launched her own quasi-television network in the summer of 2014.

But recent history suggests many precedents for her running. For one, there have been many former governors who have run for the presidency and a number of them have won (Carter in 1976, Reagan in 1980, Clinton in 1992, and George W. Bush in 2000). Also, former vice presidential candidates have a record of running, including Robert Dole in 1976, Walter Mondale in 1984, and John Edwards in 2008. While none have been victorious, the precedent for a campaign has been established. And, perhaps most importantly, Palin indicated her interest in the position into 2014. In March 2014, the *Huffington Post* reported that Palin had not ruled out a run in 2016.[11] She reportedly told Fox News Network host, Greta Van Susteren: "Now, I—at this point in time, I don't have a team of people, you know, getting out there doing these poll-tested whatever they do to let you know if you should run or not. I don't have any of that kind of organization going," but Palin cautioned, "I'll never say never."

But it is her base of support in the Tea Party that makes her such a strong contender for the movement's backing. After her 2008 loss with Senator John McCain, Palin remained active in electoral politics. Exit polling following the 2010 election conducted by *Politico* showed that she was the most popular national figure for Tea Party supporters. The poll found 15% of Tea Party supporters believed that Palin "exemplifies the goals of the Tea Party movement" and the same percentage listed her as the top candidate for the White House in 2012, ahead of Mitt Romney at the time.[12] While Palin has never formally run a Tea Party organization, she frequently appears at Tea Party events as a featured speaker. The TPE featured Palin at a 2014 rally to support Tea Party–backed New Jersey Senate candidate, Steve Lonegan. Amy Kremer, the chair of TPE, said, "We are excited to have Governor Sarah Palin join us this Saturday. The momentum for Steve Lonegan continues to grow and Governor Palin's voice will add immensely to that fact. Governor Palin has been a powerful leader for this movement and continues to spread a message that resonates with the people."[13]

And Palin also backed candidates for office. In 2010 and again in 2012, as I showed in Chapter 4, she prominently endorsed Tea Party candidates, and at least half won. In 2010, she endorsed 64 candidates, most tied to the Tea Party. She endorsed Marco Rubio (who won in Florida), Pat Toomey (who won in Pennsylvania), and Rand Paul (who won in Kentucky).[14] But she also backed several notable losers, including Joe Miller (who lost in Alaska), Christine O'Donnell (who lost in Delaware), and Sharon Angle (who lost in Nevada). Her Tea Party endorsement winning percentage was not that much different from others noted in Chapter 5, and she championed many successful women candidates for statewide office.

The strict orthodoxy imposed by the Tea Party has worked to the benefit of Palin's chances in 2016, since she has been out of office, signed no laws into effect, and not voted on any bills. Unlike Senator Marco Rubio, who cast hundreds of votes, most of which have pleased the Tea Party, but a few that have been too compromising, by remaining outside of elected office, Palin's record has remained clean, and she has taken advantage of this. On Marco Rubio, who she had supported in 2010, Palin called for him to be opposed in the 2016 Republican primaries. She told Fox News Radio: "[Rubio] has said that he would never support legalization of illegals, of those who entered and stayed in the U.S. illegally. He promised that he wouldn't support such a thing as amnesty and that border security would come first. But instead, he's reneged on that promise."[15] Distance from elected office has permitted Governor Palin the opportunity to render judgments and remain largely free of specific criticism of her policy decisions.

Palin also offers to shift the image of the Tea Party from common conceptions of the movement as almost all-white, older, and male. Given the potential for a woman to top the ticket for the Democratic Party in 2016, this adds to the appeal of Palin's profile. But as I showed in Chapter 3, on average, Tea Party women hold distinct views from Tea Party men. Tea Party women tend to be more socially conservative, much like Palin, and less libertarian. This could have an impact on who would be drawn to a Palin campaign. Whereas Rubio might draw new supporters to the Tea Party movement, Palin is likely to energize the core group of social conservative supporters, but might not inspire nonconservative Tea Party Independents and Tea Party libertarians. She was a vocal critic of Rubio's immigration plan, thus might not draw in new Hispanic American supporters either. If nothing else, as she has in the past, Sarah Palin will draw attention to the Tea Party, much of it desired and helpful, but some of it likely to do harm to the advancement of the movement.

SENATOR RAND PAUL

A third possibility for the Tea Party is Senator Rand Paul (KY). Paul offers a variety of attributes for a national run for the presidency, some that Rubio and Palin are lacking. First, Senator Paul is the son of Congressman Ron Paul, who long served as a folk hero figure for libertarians and many in the Tea Party. Next to Sarah Palin, Ron Paul is revered above all others. Ron Paul ran as a Libertarian candidate for the presidency in 1988, again for the Republican presidential nomination in 2008 and then again in 2012. Despite his losses, Ron Paul refused to endorse the eventual Republican nominations, earning him great praise as an uncompromising political purist. Ron Paul also was supported by a well-organized state political infrastructure connected to the Tea Party that helped him in early Republican contests despite having few of the financial resources afforded to his opposition. In 2012, polling showed that in Iowa, 20% of Tea Party supporters backed Paul, second to Rick Santorum, and 22% of New Hampshire Tea Party supporters later backed him.[16]

Second, Rand Paul, the son, was himself elected as a part of the Tea Party class of 2010, challenging a Republican moderate in the party primary, and then defeating his Democratic challenger. Much like Rubio, Senator Paul ushered in the second phase of the Tea Party movement with his claim to a seat in the Senate. This legacy bodes well for gaining the support of major Tea Party financial supporters in the future.

Third, once in Washington, Senator Paul pursued an unconventional legislative strategy, particularly for those affiliated with the Tea Party. Paul championed bipartisan legislation on issues such as criminal justice policy, and gained fame for a lengthy filibuster against the use of drones for which the Democrat, Senator Ron Wyden, gave support.[17] He also spoke at meetings of the National Association for the Advancement of Colored People (NAACP) to court the support of African American activists and voters. Unlike Palin, Rand Paul presented a much more ideologically eclectic face, supporting issues with crossover appeal, and also with less of a focus on socially conservative issues.

Fourth, and probably most importantly, Paul is popular with different groups of voters and in key states. CNN polling in 2014 found that Paul topped the list of favored Republican candidates for the White House in 2016.[18] He earned 16% of the support, just ahead of Congressman Paul Ryan (15%) and Senator Marco Rubio (5%). He also received the most support from Independents (22%), the largest percentage of all the Republican candidates. In Iowa and New Hampshire, polling in 2014 found that Paul was either on top or tied for first, a sign that he has support in the more social conservative Midwest and also in the more libertarian-oriented Northeast.[19]

POTENTIAL TEA PARTY CANDIDATES AND CAMPAIGN FINANCE

As Chapters 4 and 5 demonstrated, money has become increasingly important in political campaigns. While total dollars raised and spent may not explain everything about who wins and who loses, it is hard to imagine a candidate who would be able to mount a run for the presidency in 2016 without the backing of several billion dollars. Each of the potential Tea Party candidates for the presidency has different histories of fund-raising and campaign spending. By comparing the three, we can get a better understanding of the viability of a run for the presidency.

Politicians raise money in a variety of ways. Most raise money through political action committees (PACs), which are further classified as campaign committees (which primarily support the politicians' own election ambitions and secondarily those of other candidates) and leadership committees (which primarily allow the politician to support other candidates). In the House, contributions are limited to $5,000 per candidate per election for leadership PACs and $2,000 per candidate, per election for campaign committees.[20] These are not terribly important distinctions to understand how effective each candidate is, but these are terms used to categorize how Palin, Paul, and Rubio each have raised money.

Sarah Palin has not run for office since 2008, so she has not had a campaign committee, but as noted earlier, she has been involved in electoral politics and is known to be a prolific fund-raiser. She created SarahPAC, a leadership PAC that has donated money to candidates for office. In 2010, for example, SarahPAC raised nearly $6 million ($5.68 million to be exact), according to the Center for Responsive Politics, and spent over $4.3 million.[21] This placed the PAC just outside the top 20 in terms of PAC receipts. SarahPAC supported a variety of candidates in 2010, including $7,000 given to Rand Paul and $5,000 to Marco Rubio, and was second only to the leadership PAC for Mitt Romney for contributions to candidates. In 2012, SarahPAC was again active, raising and spending around $5 million, making contributions only to Republican candidates. It is clear that one of Sarah Palin's chief political assets is her ability to fund-raise.

Marco Rubio has also been an effective fund-raiser. Between the time he ran for office and 2014, he and his supporters raised $29.6 million in a variety of ways.[22] Rubio established a leadership PAC called Reclaim America PAC that raised $1.9 million in 2012 and $3.2 million in 2014. And Rubio Victory Committee raised $9.2 million, second only to the committee supporting House Speaker John Boehner, despite Rubio not being up for reelection in 2014. On the contrary, Rand Paul Victory Committee raised just $1.4 million in 2014. Since he ran for office, Paul raised a total $13 million. Paul's leadership PAC, Reinventing a New Direction, raised $1.9 million in 2012 and then $2.5 million in 2014.

Given the rising role of outside money in politics, whoever runs for office in 2016 will likely be indirectly aided by millions of largely unregulated independent expenditures for which they will never have to ask. Nevertheless, fund-raising is still important for individual candidates as it shows certain things about the level of support among wealthy donors. Much more so than Rand Paul, Sarah Palin, and Marco Rubio have strong records of fund-raising prowess that they would bring to the presidential campaign in 2016.

POTENTIAL TEA PARTY CANDIDATES AND CABLE NEWS COVERAGE

Marco Rubio, Sarah Palin, and Rand Paul are qualified candidates for the presidency, in part, because of their ability to raise money, but also the role they have played in the advancement of the Tea Party. Each has been supported by the Tea Party and, in return, they have each played a role in advancing the Tea Party on the national stage. By the spring of 2015, two—Rubio and Paul—had officially entered the Republican race. But, as Chapter 4 showed, the media has also played a part in supporting the Tea Party. The analysis in that chapter built on previous research on the amount of coverage major television cable news stations have given to the movement. We learned from that analysis about the ebbs and flows of coverage across CNN, Fox News, and MSNBC. Have these three prominent Tea Party leaders been covered in the same way? Or has the amount of cable news coverage differed? I used the same method from Chapter 4 to catalogue Tea Party coverage for each of these three potential candidates and graphed that over time (see Figure 6.1).[23]

From these data, we can observe some of the changing patterns of Tea Party support for each candidate that I just described earlier mirrored in

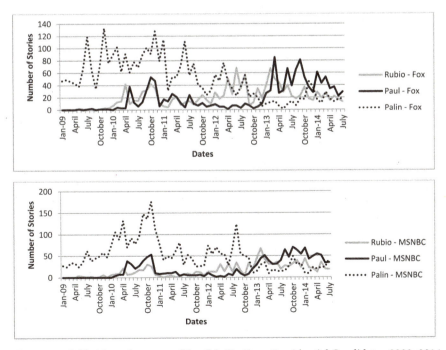

Figure 6.1 Cable News Coverage of Possible Tea Party Presidential Candidates, 2009–2014 (Original analysis using Lexis-Nexis)

cable news coverage. The first thing we can see is that, coming off of the 2008 loss as the Republican Party's vice presidential candidate, Sarah Palin remained a prominent subject of both Fox News and MSNBC. Through the first year of the Tea Party, the coverage for Palin dwarfed that for Rubio and Paul. At that point, neither of the two future senators had declared their intent to run for the Senate, thus neither had the national stature to demand news coverage. Palin maintained the central position in the Tea Party, while the others were likely unknown to anyone outside of their home states.

Second, as we approached the 2010 election and then transitioned to the second phase of the Tea Party movement, Rubio and Paul began to gather news coverage. While both were largely left out of extensive coverage during the first phase, Rubio in particular drew interest in late 2011 and into 2012. On Fox News, the coverage of Rubio nearly supplanted Palin by the time of the 2012 presidential election. Recall that Rubio was strongly considered as a running mate to the Governor Mitt Romney, and he gave a major speech at the Republican National Convention in Tampa, Florida.

Third, Palin's coverage continued to dwindle on both Fox News and MSNBC at the same time Senator Paul's coverage expanded. Starting in January 2013, Rand Paul received the most coverage from Fox News and from MSNBC. Paul emerged during this time as the central figure of the three and increasingly as a national political figure. Fourth, whereas the coverage of Senator Rubio spiked in the middle part of the second phase of the Tea Party movement, the coverage faded away as we moved toward the summer of 2014. Rubio's difficulties with immigration reform occurred at the same time his media coverage dwindled. At the writing of this book, based on the amount of media coverage, Senator Rand Paul's star is rising, as the two others are falling.

Who ultimately runs for the White House in 2016 will come down to many factors, including the ability to maintain positive coverage in the news and also to raise money, but in Rubio, Palin, and Paul, the Tea Party has three potential candidates to consider. Each has strong ties to the earliest days of the Tea Party, thus can speak with a degree of legitimacy about being a part of the Tea Party in a way that other candidates like Governor Jeb Bush and Governor Chris Christie cannot.[24] But each of the three poses issues for the Tea Party. Rubio's advocacy for immigration reform, Palin's allegiance to a moderate presidential candidate in 2008, and Paul's forays into bipartisan legislation rub against key tenets of the movement. To truly back one of the three, the uncompromising tendencies of the Tea Party would need to be placed to the side in the favor of consensus. If the Tea Party ultimately backs one of these three candidates, then the third phase of the Tea Party will be characterized by a very different politics than the previous two. A run for the presidency could see the Tea Party mature into a much more mainstream political movement, than it was in the past. A Tea Party candidate for the president could bring a degree of unity to the movement that was largely absent from the first two phases. And, of course, if a Tea Party candidate won, the movement would be granted the widespread legitimacy that it lacked early on.

If, on the other hand, consensus cannot be found between one of these three and none of the three run, then the third phase may look a lot like the second phase. Figuring out whether to support a traditional Republican candidate, such as South Dakota senator John Thune or Congressman Paul Ryan, or whether to back a long-shot Libertarian candidate would likely see Tea Party organizations and activists continue to grapple with the identity of the movement. Rather than grow in legitimacy, the third phase might see the movement continue to lose support and organized opposition from mainstream conservative groups, like the Chamber of Commerce, could push Tea Party organizations further to the margins.

BROADENING THE MESSAGE

Whether it is Paul, Palin, or Rubio, or simply a more general focus on the presidential race, national-level electoral politics offers one future for the Tea Party. Another direction for the third phase of the Tea Party would be a return to home. When I interviewed Tea Party activists in Roanoke, Virginia, in the summer of 2014, they expressed frustration with the direction the movement had taken. Recall from Chapter 5 that the Roanoke Tea Party had been thrown out of a statewide federation of Tea Party organizations, in part because of the politics of a burgeoning run for the U.S. Senate by another Tea Party leader in the state. Many of its efforts to push for change in state laws, including what was called nullification, had been frustrated by the increasingly national policy aims of the Virginia Tea Party Federation. In part a result, Greg Aldridge explained that his organization has shifted its strategy to a much more local focus. His group began focusing on local races for city council and other municipal offices. He also said that issues such as indefinite detention, agricultural and farming freedom, and medical marijuana, issues he believed had resonance with the antiestablishment Left, could emerge in the future. The group is also looking ahead and prioritizing basic education issues by traveling to local schools and teaching about the freedoms protected by the Constitution.

Not every Tea Party organization has given up on national elections, but there are reasons to believe that the effort to find common cause with those outside the Tea Party might show promise for the movement. And there is a precedent for this type of shift in previous social movements. Kristin Goss showed that the women's movement regained its power in Washington as it "broadened its agenda in the 1980s" by "highlighting the ways in which broader issues such as the economy and Social Security affected women."[25] By broadening its agenda, the women's movement could expand its base of supporters, many of whom had been shut out of the movement because of its narrow agenda in the past.

Scholars have also remarked on this possible direction. Hans Noel contended that Tea Party could reach out to libertarian issues to broaden its appeal: "The Tea Party could find allies on the left on some issues. Some Tea Party activists with libertarian leanings might find some common cause with Vermont Senator Bernie Sanders."[26] During the summer of 2014, one particular policy issue emerged that offered such a path and rallied supporters of the Tea Party: the Export-Import Bank. The obscurity of the policy issue did not detract from the attention it got from organizations linked to the Tea Party, including the Club for Growth.

EXPORT-IMPORT BANK

The Export-Import Bank issue aligned closely with an organizing principle of the Tea Party: opposition to what was deemed "corporate welfare." Recall that Rick Santelli's rant on CNBC was, at least, in part directed at federal bailouts given to certain businesses and banks. For some in the Tea Party, the Export-Import Bank represented an analogous situation of crony capitalism and government support for certain companies that ran counter to a belief about the free market.

The Export-Import Bank was established in the 1930s, reauthorized by Democrats and Republicans alike ever since, and in 2014 had a mission to "assist in financing the export of U.S. goods and services to international markets" by providing "export financing products that fill gaps in trade financing . . . provides working capital guarantees (pre-export financing); export credit insurance; and loan guarantees and direct loans (buyer financing)."[27] To be sure, the bank is a relatively small operation in relation to the overall size of the federal government. It mainly supports U.S. businesses, but some aid goes to foreign companies interested in purchasing U.S. goods and services.

As early as 2013, Tea Party advocates began to mobilize against the bank. The Tea Party Patriots (TPP) posted on its blog information from the Club for Growth about the nomination of the new head of the bank, Fred Hochberg. The TPP wrote: "This is what President Obama is supporting with his support for Hochberg—crony capitalism, egregious violations of the free market, and a gross waste of your tax dollars. Supporters claim your tax dollars are necessary to protect American companies from subsidies and protections by other countries, but shouldn't the federal government attempt to convince those countries to be more free-market oriented, not encourage further corruption inside our own borders?"[28] The post continued that activists could "bombard Senators at their Washington offices and in their district offices with letters and phone calls. Show up at town halls. Write letters to the editor and op-eds in your local, regional, and statewide newspapers and popular political websites. Make sure your Senators know that you stand against crony capitalism, that you stand for the ethical use of your tax dollars, and that you will hold them accountable." While the Export-Import Bank was a tiny piece of the federal budget, and its dismantling would offer few savings, since it arguably generated more revenue than it took in federal spending, the Tea Party could still frame this as a principled stand. The Export-Import Bank could represent the disgust with political corruption that the Tea Party labeled as "crony capitalism." And TPP aimed to use many of the same outside tactics that worked so well to foment public attention in the first phase, including mass mobilizing, protesting, and attendance at public events. FreedomWorks and other Tea Party groups also came out against the bank.

The Tea Party effort to derail the Hochberg nomination failed, but a year later the bank issue arose again at the tail end of the second phase of the Tea Party movement because of its sunsetting congressional mandate. In 2002, President George W. Bush, signed and announced: "I have today signed into law S. 1372, the Export-Import Bank Reauthorization Act of 2002. This legislation will ensure the continued effective operation of the Export-Import Bank, which helps advance U.S. trade policy, facilitate the sale of U.S. goods and services abroad, and create jobs here at home."[29] The bank's congressional authorization was due to run out on September 30, 2014, necessitating legislative action to extend its charter.

As the Tea Party, and allies such as the Club for Growth, ramped up opposition again, the Chamber of Commerce and National Association of Manufacturers, two longtime allies of the Republican Party, aimed to defend the bank and maintain the programs the bank supports.[30] These industry representatives, whose members had benefited from the activities of the bank over the previous 80 years, fought back against the Tea Party efforts to close the bank. As we saw in Chapter 4, U.S. industry was not always an enthusiastic supporter of the Tea Party, particularly during the second phase.

The Export-Import Bank reauthorization, thus, was another issue that drove a wedge between different wings of the Republican Party, but in doing so, it opened a potential door to new allies. In general, the American public had lost faith in big business at about the same rate as it had with the government. Gallup showed that between 2002 and 2012, satisfaction with the "size and power" of the federal government dipped from 60% down to 31%, and for major corporations from 50% down to 29%.[31] Progressives and liberals have long opposed the same type of crony capitalism that the Tea Party abhors. The progressive titan, Ralph Nader, and the organizations he has founded, Public Citizen and Public Interest Research Groups (PIRG), have fought against the preferential treatment of U.S. businesses and corporate welfare since the 1960s. The Export-Import Bank issue opened a door for the Tea Party to potential supporters on the Left who agree that crony capitalism is a problem and federal support for banks and businesses in need of reform.

But this common cause formed with the Left has some obvious limitations, especially because of other prominent parts of the progressive agenda focused on corporate welfare, specifically the role of money in politics. Attacking the tiny Export-Import Bank might be an area of agreement, but given what we learned in Chapter 4, major changes in the way political campaigns are funded, new restrictions on lobbying, and ridding politics of money would likely be nonstarters for the Tea Party. In each case, the Tea Party would likely chafe at the impositions on freedoms and liberty inherent to each of these campaign finance reform policy proposals.

COMMON CORE CURRICULUM

Another policy issue that increasingly drew the attention of the Tea Party was the Common Core curriculum. As with the Export-Import Bank, the Common Core has been supported by a bipartisan coalition of state associations, like the Council of Chief State School Officers (CCSSO) and the National Governors Association, and businesses, such as Boeing, Dell, and GlaxoSmithKline. But unlike the Export-Import Bank, the Common Core has not been legislated in Congress, and the direct impact of the reform is in local schools. Advocates of the Common Core describe it as "a set of high-quality academic standards in mathematics and English language arts/literacy (ELA)" that "define the knowledge and skills students should gain throughout their K-12 education in order to graduate high school prepared to succeed in entry level careers, introductory academic college courses, and workforce training programs."[32] They also focus on the Common Core being a "state-led effort" that was informed by the feedback from thousands of parents and citizens since 2009. It is voluntary for states to use the curriculum, but nearly all states (43 as of July 2014), the District of Columbia, and several other entities adopted the standards.

There has been wide and diverse support for the Common Core, but Tea Party opposition appeared as well. Some of the elements of the Common Core contrasted with an original Tea Party belief about states' rights and local control. Federal dictates have always been an anathema to the Tea Party, and new national mandates about what would or would not be taught in local schools connected to this antifederal ethos, even if these claims may have been were exaggerated. To be sure, the Common Core is not mandated by the federal government, nor was it developed by federal policymakers at the Department of Education. Nevertheless, opponents have painted it as an effort to further federalize education policy and create a National School Board. This framing drew Tea Party activists to join in opposition to the implementation of the new curricular strategy.

The opposition to the Common Core also aligns with those possessing few previous connections to the Tea Party. More left-wing or progressive organizations have long opposed standardization of education, high-stakes testing, and taking control of the curriculum out of the hands of teachers.[33] Diane Ravitch, the Network for Public Education, and the U.S. Coalition for World Class Math opposed the Common Core. Much like the case of the Export-Import Bank, these organizations offer to the Tea Party a chance to pull in new organizational assets and support from parts of the country that they have been missing in the second phase.

An issue, such as the Common Core curriculum, offers the Tea Party a way to find new organizational allies, but also new supporters. Around the issue of local control, there are pockets of individuals associated with the Democratic Party, libertarians, and also Independents who may find education issues an area to support the Tea Party. And unlike opposing the debt ceiling or even the Export-Import Bank, where the issues are ambiguous and impacts indirect, potential supporters of the Tea Party will have firsthand experiences with classroom curriculum. Opposition to the Common Core curriculum fits with the local turn taken by the Roanoke Tea Party and with the local roots of the Tea Party movement in its first phase.

MEDICAL MARIJUANA

Another policy arena that the Tea Party movement could rejuvenate and rally support is over the issue of medical marijuana usage and drug legalization. Libertarians—including Ron Paul—and the Libertarian Party have long campaigned on these issues, especially as an issue that states, not the federal government, should legislate, but the Tea Party has been slower to embrace cannabis. Organizations, like the Columbia (SC) Tea Party, contended that they are "only concerned with issues relating to our three core values of fiscal responsibility, limited government, and adherence to the U.S. Constitution. We do not take sides on any social issues such as abortion, gay marriage, or marijuana legalization."[34] This is typical of the approach of many Tea Party organizations who rarely even acknowledge the issue. The failure to take a stand on marijuana issues is also related to the socially conservative side of the Tea Party that has largely rejected these policy positions. But when the marijuana issue is framed as a states' rights issue, one can see the clear opening for the endorsement of the Tea Party.[35]

Moreover, support for various drug legalization issues, including the loosening of laws related to the medical use of marijuana, may allow for bonds to be formed with the Left. Public opinion polling confirms that this could be a winning strategy for the Tea Party. A poll conducted by Reason-Rupe showed that while a majority (55%) of Democrats and Independents support marijuana legalization, more than a third (38%) of Tea Party supporters do, compared to just a quarter (27%) of Republicans.[36] This comparatively larger amount of support among Tea Party supporters suggests there is a ground for the larger movement to pursue the issue. And even among Republicans, in general, nearly three-quarters (72%) believe that marijuana has legitimate medical uses, and 61% support medical marijuana laws.[37]

And this unusual common cause across partisan lines has already appeared in Washington. John Hudak of the Brookings analyzed votes taken on an amendment introduced to direct the Drug Enforcement Administration (DEA) to stop enforcing federal law in states that had passed medical marijuana laws.[38] Hudak showed that all of the Democrats in the House voted for the amendment, but since they were in the minority, Republicans were also needed to pass the bill. The Republicans who ultimately voted for the bill, though, were not moderates, but instead mainly conservative members of the Tea Party Caucus, including Congressman Justin Amash (MI) and Mick Mulvaney (SC). Hudak concluded: "Conservatives see this issue as one of states' rights and a means of reducing the role of federal influence. After spending years criticizing ObamaCare as government coming between a patient and her doctor, Republicans see prohibitions on medical marijuana as similar interference. Pushing the feds to take a hands-off approach is consistent with both liberal and Tea Party ideologies." Not to be too late to the game, Senator Rand Paul introduced a similar amendment in the Senate shortly after the bill passed in the House.[39]

Further from Washington, local Tea Party organizations and candidates have also started to support medical marijuana laws. In Georgia, the leader of the Atlanta Tea Party, Julianne Thompson, testified in support of a state law that would permit limited medical uses of marijuana.[40] And in California, a Tea Party Republican candidate, Igor Birman, was endorsed by the

Marijuana Policy Project, one of the leading advocacy groups on the issue, because of his supportive stance on marijuana issues.[41]

Any policy issue that is backed by an ever-growing percentage of voters of all partisan stripes will be considered, if not endorsed, by major political parties. Since the issue of medical marijuana also aligns with concerns about personal liberty and states' rights, it seems a natural one for the Tea Party to take up. If the Tea Party organizers see the third phase as the time to form a broader coalition, rather than to rally around a small policy agenda of cutting taxes and limiting government spending, then medical marijuana makes additional sense. But in pursuing this strategy, the divisions within the Tea Party, particularly those between social conservatives and libertarians, will either have to be negotiated or some within the Tea Party may depart for other political camps. The same difficult compromises will likely have to be reached if issues like the Common Core curriculum and the Export-Import Bank continue to place the Tea Party in opposition to traditional conservative interests. A renegade strategy that opens doors to other antiestablishment interests, especially those on the far Left, could invigorate the Tea Party and mobilize a new generation of supporters. But in pursuing this strategy during the third phase, it might make winning future elections and gaining national policy victories a harder and harder ambition.

CONCLUDING THOUGHTS

The diversity of ways to define the Tea Party renders predictions about the future highly uncertain. This book has argued, rather than previous explanations of the Tea Party as just one thing or another, that the divisions within the Tea Party explain the most about the movement. Important differences existed between the types of organizations that formed in 2009, some small local organizations and others large national groups, and the strategies and tactics they pursued, sometimes insider and sometimes outsider. Differences also emerged between the various people of the Tea Party, with several distinct camps of Tea Party being conservative Republicans, Tea Party libertarians, and even Tea Party Democrats.

These differences in the people and the organizations of the Tea Party shifted from the first to the second phase of the movement. In the second phase, Tea Party organizations became more professionalized and adopted strategies focused more on the internal politics of Washington, rather than the external politics of organizing and protesting. The second phase saw dozens of Tea Party members of Congress arrive in Washington. While they have been labeled as obstructionists and described as uncompromising, the members of the Tea Party class of 2010 were hardly unified. These new members of Congress usually voted with the Republican majority, but often this meant in opposition to the wishes of the biggest backers of the Tea Party. The very different legislative paths pursued by Justin Amash, Raul Labrador, Vicky Jo Hartzler, and David McKinley attest to the divisions within the Tea Party.

These second phase shifts in strategy led some to conclude that the movement, in fact, never was based at the grassroots; rather it was simply the latest in a long tradition of top-down conservative movements. The argument about the Astroturf nature of the Tea Party has several compelling points, including the overwhelming financial largesse of figures like the Koch brothers, and the support the movement received from coverage on the Fox News Network. But these arguments have been overstated. Research shows that Fox News did not cover the Tea Party that much differently than other outlets, and MSNBC was much more critical than Fox News was glowing. And to make this Astroturf argument is to minimize the work of thousands of activists to form small Tea Party organizations across the country, and to apply a reductionist approach to the movement's history. I argue in this book that the Tea Party was, and is likely to remain, diverse: both a grassroots and elite-based movement, both libertarian and social conservative, both revolutionary and also deeply conventional. It is a diverse and complex political phenomenon that does not lend itself to a single explanation, thus understanding the diversity and divisions will prove most effective.

We can also learn a lot about politics in general from this understanding of the Tea Party. The Tea Party was alike political movements of the past in certain ways. The movement expressed a political viewpoint that was out of the mainstream and that had not been central to the agendas of either of the two major political parties in the country. The women's movement, the environmental movement, and the peace movement all began at the fringes of politics, and slowly moved to the center through organizing, mobilizing, and later success in electoral politics. The early history of the Tea Party was largely the same.

But the Tea Party movement has also been different. First, the speed of the movement distinguishes it from the past. Nearly a thousand organizations of various types formed within just a few months. This is unprecedented in U.S. history. Second, one explanation for this speed is the role of technology. As I showed in Chapter 2, digital technology, the Internet, and social media shaped the Tea Party movement in a way that earlier movements were not. The opportunity to create websites quickly and inexpensively, to connect hundreds of thousands of supporters together in a network, and to share information directly helped propel the Tea Party ahead faster than earlier technologies had for movements in the past. Third, another explanation for this speed is the role of money. As Chapter 4 showed, the Tea Party arose during a period of the rapidly ascending role of money in politics. The Tea Party was both a player and beneficiary of this shift. Previous political movements depended on patrons and financial support, but never before has a political movement been so closely associated with so much money. Previous political movements, though often supported by patrons, largely operated at the financial fringe of politics. For the Tea Party, money rapidly moved its organizations and candidates to the center of politics.

Some of these factors are unique to the Tea Party and the political moment of the early days of the Obama administration, but others will define future political movements. Technology and money are unlikely to wane in importance in U.S. politics. Unless there are great changes in the composition of the Supreme Court, the U.S. Constitution will continue to open doors for individuals to use money to participate in politics. In this political environment, future activists and organizers will grapple with how to gain access to patrons, while at the same time confronting the inherent conflicts of accepting monetary support. Tea Party organizers in towns and cities, who barely benefited from the support of the Koch brothers and their associated organizations, still confronted the accusation that they were simply pawns in a larger political game. Future political activists will suffer from these same accusations if they cannot maintain control over their message while gathering the support of professional political players and financial backers. One solution, one I argue for in this chapter, is a move by the Tea Party back to the local roots. The national stage of politics may always be prone to the oversized influence of a small number of donors and interests, but local politics may remain a fertile ground for smaller political movements to gain traction. Whether it is around issues of education reform or drug legalization, local politics may define the next phase of the Tea Party, and be the home of future political movements, some deeply hostile to the Tea Party, others working in common cause.

Common cause will never be reached between supporters of the Tea Party, or whatever it is called in the future, and other political interests if the issue of race remains unresolved or underestimated. The election of the first African American president coincided with the rise of the Tea Party, and we cannot fully disentangle the two. President Obama's race was a prominent aspect of his presidency: it informed his agenda and the way the country responded to his leadership. The president's race also shaped the Tea Party, but not just in the deeply racist slogans and costumes at certain rallies. Race shaped the agenda of the Tea Party, even as many activists claimed they were color blind. The antigovernment and pro-states' rights core of many Tea Party organizations linked them to a legacy of segregation and a history of institutionalized discrimination. Tea Party activists likely dispute such a claim, arguing instead that they have no more connection to the John Birch Society or the Klu Klux Klan than any other organization. But to deny that politics and political movements are rooted in history is to grossly misrepresent U.S. politics. Tea Party organizations relied on many of the same arguments and tactics that were developed decades earlier. This was not a coincidence, since we know many of the same patrons who supported those ideas long ago supported the Tea Party. For the Tea Party to remain a vibrant political movement and fully participate in politics in the future, leaders and activists need to confront this legacy. We really do not know whether the majority of Tea Party leaders are any more racist than political leaders of other organizations, but there is a particular burden on future Tea Party leaders to be outspoken critics of racism, to vocally denounce supporters who spout bigotry, and to open the movement to a broad range of the public. If the beliefs in personal liberty and freedom are true convictions, Tea Party leaders should find ways to advance civil liberties and to protect a wider array of freedoms, than they have in the past. Failing to address the issue of race in the Tea Party will likely mean its tenure as a political movement will not outlast the second term of President Obama.

For the movement's financial patrons, the dismantling of the Tea Party would likely not be surprising nor viewed as a particular loss. Patrons, such as the Koch brothers, operated long before the rise of the Tea Party and will certainly persist if the Tea Party goes away. Patrons will identify new symbols, support new organizations, and advance a similar agenda, just with a new set of names. This would be a great loss, since a future movement may not have the grassroots elements that defined a part of the Tea Party. As money becomes ever more prominent in U.S. politics, political patrons may see fewer and fewer reasons to ally themselves with the type of organizing and local activism that defined the first phase of the Tea Party. At the very least, the Tea Party movement has been a mix of grassroots activism and elite-based Astroturfing. The same cannot be said about future movements. This would do harm to the democracy and potentially to the individuals rights and liberties in which thousands of Tea Party activists believed so strongly.

Notes

CHAPTER 1

1. Mark Meckler and Jenny Beth Martin, *Tea Party Patriots: The Second American Revolution* (New York: Henry Holt and Co, 2012).

2. "Nationwide 'Tea Party' Protests Blast Spreading," CNN, April 15, 2009, http://www.cnn.com/2009/POLITICS/04/15/tea.parties/; "Signs of the Tea Party Protests," *Time*, April 2009, http://content.time.com/time/photogallery/0,29307,1922169,00.html; "Tea Party: More Signs of Racism?" *Mother Jones*, September,28,2010,http://www.motherjones.com/slideshows/2010/09/tea-partys-racist-signs/niggar.

3. Theda Skocpol and Vanessa Williamson, *The Tea Party and the Remaking of Republican Conservatism* (New York: Oxford University Press, 2012).

4. Ronald Formissano, *The Tea Party: A Brief History* (Baltimore, MD: Johns Hopkins University Press, 2012).

5. Skocpol and Williamson, *The Tea Party and the Remaking of Republican Conservatism*, 184.

6. Anthony DiMaggio, *The Rise of the Tea Party* (New York: New York University Press, 2011), 10.

7. Ian Haney Lopez, *Dog Whistle Politics: How Coded Racial Appeals Have Reinvented Racism and Wrecked the Middle Class* (New York: Oxford University Press, 2014).

8. Doug McAdam and Karina Kloos, *Deeply Divided: Racial Politics and Social Movements in Postwar America* (New York: Oxford University Press, 2014).

9. Joseph Lowndes, "The Past and Future of Race in the Tea Party Movement," in *Steep: The Precipitous Rise of the Tea Party*, ed. Christine Trost and Lawrence Rosenthal (Berkeley: University of California Press, 2012), 171–192.

10. Alan Abramowitz, "Grand Old Tea Party. The Tea Parties in Historical Perspective: A Conservative Response to a Crisis of Political Economy," in *Steep: The Precipitous Rise of the Tea Party*, ed. Christine Trost and Lawrence Rosenthal (Berkeley: University of California Press, 2012), 195–211.

11. Meckler and Martin, *Tea Party Patriots*.

12. Robert Horwitz, *America's Right: Anti-establishment Conservatism from Goldwater to the Tea Party* (Malden, MA: Polity Press, 2013).

13. Eric Hoffer, *The True Believer: Thoughts on the Nature of Mass Movements* (New York: Harper & Row, 1951).

14. Horwitz, *America's Right*, 166.

15. George Michael, "The Tea Party and the Far Right: Fellow Travelers?" in *Extremism in America*, ed. George Michael (Gainesville: University of Florida Press, 2014), 28.

16. Kristin Goss, *The Paradox of Gender Equality: How American Women's Groups Gained and Lost Their Public Voice* (Ann Arbor: University of Michigan Press, 2013).

17. Clarence Lo, "AstroTurf versus Grass Roots: Scenes from Early Tea Party Mobilization," in *Steep: The Precipitous Rise of the Tea Party*, ed. Christine Trost and Lawrence Rosenthal (Berkeley: University of California Press, 2012), 98–130.

18. Glenn Feldman, "Introduction," in *Nation within A Nation: The American South and the Federal Government*, ed. Glenn Feldman (Gainesville: University of Florida Press), 1–18.

19. E. E. Schattschneider, *The Semi-Sovereign People* (New York: Holt, Reinhart, and Winston, 1960).

CHAPTER 2

1. Alexis de Tocqueville, *Democracy in America* (New York: The Century Company, 1898).

2. To conduct this aspect of the research, I relied upon the Wayback Machine, a virtual archive of millions of websites from 1996 to the present. The Wayback Machine has regularly crawled the Internet in order to save virtual copies of websites. For most websites, they maintain a nearly perfect copy of content on the website at weekly or sometimes monthly intervals. This archive is not perfect, since certain website functions are difficult to archive. But, with notable exceptions, there is not a better resource for historical research on the Internet and how websites have changed overtime. I used the Wayback Machine to collect qualitative and quantitative information from the websites of key Tea Party organizations starting in February 2009. It is worth nothing that the database is fully accessible to the public and researchers, and can be accessed at http://www.archive.org.

3. Olivier Zunz, *Philanthropy in America: A History* (Princeton, NJ: Princeton University Press, 2014).

4. Jeffrey Berry and David Arons, *A Voice for Nonprofits* (Washington, DC: Brookings Institution Press, 2003); Heath Brown, Jeffrey R. Henig, Thomas

Holyoke, and Natalie Lacierno-Paquet, "Scale of Operations and Locus of Control in Market Versus Mission-Oriented Charter Schools," *Social Science Quarterly* 85, no. 4 (2004): 1035–1051.

5. Charles Postel, "The Tea Parties in Historical Perspective: A Conservative Response to a Crisis of Political Economy," in *Steep: The Precipitous Rise of the Tea Party*, eds. Christine Trost and Lawrence Rosenthal (Berkeley: University of California Press, 2012).

6. Jack Walker, *Mobilizing Interest Groups in America: Patrons, Professionals, and Social Movements* (Ann Arbor: University of Michigan Press, 1991).

7. Edward Walker, *Grassroots for Hire: Public Affairs Consultants in American Democracy* (Cambridge: Cambridge University Press, 2014).

8. Walker, *Mobilizing Interest Groups*, 104.

9. Ibid., 105.

10. Walker, *Grassroots for Hire*, 55.

11. Skocpol and Williamson, *The Tea Party and the Remaking of Republican Conservatism*.

12. Ibid., 90.

13. Ibid.

14. Vanessa Williamson, Theda Skocpol, and John Coggin," The Tea Party and the Remaking of Republican Conservatism," *Perspectives on Politics* 9, no. 1 (2011): 25–43.

15. Ibid., n.p.

16. Devin Burghart, "The Status of Tea Party Movement: Membership, Support, and Sympathy by the Numbers," IREHR, January 24, 2014, http://www.irehr.org/issue-areas/tea-party-nationalism/tea-party-news-and-analysis/item/527-status-of-tea-party-by-the-numbers.

17. "An Up-close Look at the Tea Party and Its Role in the Midterm Elections," *The Washington Post*, October 24, 2010, http://www.washingtonpost.com/wp-srv/special/politics/tea-party-canvass/.

18. Virgil Ian Stanford, "A Tea Party Online: A Content Analysis of Local, Regional and State Tea Party Websites," *Online Journal of Communication and Media Technologies* 4, no. 3 (2014): 14.

19. Wendy Tam Cho, James Gimpel, and Daron Shaw, "The Tea Party and the Geography of Collective Action," *Quarterly Journal of Political Science* 7, no. 2 (2012): 105–133.

20. Ibid., 130.

21. Jeffrey Berry, Sarah Sobieraj, and Suzanne Schlossberg, "Tea Party Mobilization" (Presented at the American Political Science Association. New Orleans, LA, 2012).

22. To read the organization's IRS documents, go to: http://www.guidestar.org/.

23. David Karpf, *The Move-On Effect: The Unexpected Transformation of American Political Advocacy* (New York: Oxford University Press, 2012), 140.

24. Mark Meckler and Jenny Beth Martin, *Tea Party Patriots: The Second American Revolution* (New York: Henry Holt and Co, 2012).

25. Ibid.

26. Meckler and Martin, *Tea Party Patriots.*

27. Jennifer Stromer-Galley, *Presidential Campaigning in the Internet Age* (New York: Oxford University Press, 2014); Melissa Merry, "Emotional Appeals in Environmental Group Communications," *American Politics Research* 38, no. 5 (2010): 862–889.

28. Ben Smith, "Tea Party Civil War," *Politico*, November 12, 2009, http://www.politico.com/blogs/bensmith/1109/Tea_Party_civil_war.html?showall.

29. See https://web.archive.org/web/20101111175011/http://www.teapartypatriots.org/mission.aspx

30. See: http://www.freedomworks.org/.

31. Dick Armey and Matt Kibbe, "A Tea Party Manifesto," *Wall Street Journal*, August 17, 2010, http://online.wsj.com/articles/SB10001424052748704407804575425061553154540.

32. To view the archived website, see: https://web.archive.org/web/20090511081330/http://www.teapartyexpress.org/about/index.html.

33. To view the data, see: https://www.opensecrets.org/pacs/expenditures.php?cmte=C00454074&cycle=2010.

34. Helen Kennedy, "Tea Party Express Leader Mark Williams Kicked Out Over 'Colored People' Letter," *New York Daily News*, July 18, 2010, http://www.nydailynews.com/news/politics/tea-party-express-leader-mark-williams-kicked-colored-people-letter-article-1.438854.

35. To view the archived website, see: https://web.archive.org/web/20101221123409/http://www.patriotactionnetwork.com/?

36. Kate Zernike, "Convention Is Trying to Harness Tea Party Spirit," *New York Times*, February 5, 2010: A3, http://www.nytimes.com/2010/02/06/us/politics/06teaparty.html?_r=0:

37. Devin Burghart and Leonard Zeskin, "Tea Party Nationalism," *NAACP* Fall, 2010, http://naacp.3cdn.net/36b2014e1dddfe3c81_v7m6bls07.pdf.

38. Stephanie Mencimer, "Walker Campaign Disavows Controversial Tea Party Group," *Mother Jones*, June 4, 2012, http://www.motherjones.com/mojo/2012/06/discredited-tea-party-group-claims-scott-walker-sponsorship.

39. Alex Seitz-Wald, "Analysis: Taxed Enough Already? Tea Party Rallies Significantly Smaller This Year Than Last," *Think Progress*, April 19, 2011, http://thinkprogress.org/politics/2011/04/19/159516/tea-party-rallies-getting-smaller/.

40. Skocpol and Williamson, *The Tea Party*, 98.

41. Alan McBride, "Tax Fury and the Tea party: The Tea Party in the South: Populism Revisited?" in *Nation within a Nation: The American South and the Federal Government*, ed. G. Feldman (Gainesville: University of Florida Press, 2014), 317.

42. Berry et al., "Tea Party Mobilization," 31.

43. Isaac Martin, *The Rich People's Movements: Grassroots Campaigns to Untax the One Percent* (New York: Oxford University Press, 2013).

CHAPTER 3

1. Cory Dillard, "Leaving the Tea Party," *The Virginia Pilot* Online, October 8, 2013, http://hamptonroads.com/2013/10/leaving-tea-party.

2. Dara Strolovitch, "Do Interest Groups Represent the Disadvantaged? Advocacy at the Intersection of Race, Class, and Gender," The Journal of Politics 68, no. 4 (2006): 893–908.

3. Matt Grossmann, *The Not-So-Special Interests: Interest Groups, Public Representation, and American Governance* (Palo Alto, CA: Stanford University Press, 2012).

4. Ibid., 71.

5. Christopher Parker and Matthew Barreto, *Change They Can't Believe In: The Tea Party and Reactionary Politics in America* (Princeton, NJ: Princeton University Press, 2013); Abramowitz, "Grand Old Tea Party," 195–211.

6. To read the data from Gallup, see: http://www.gallup.com/poll/147635/tea-party-movement.aspx.

7. To read the data full Gallup, see: http://www.gallup.com/poll/141512/congress-ranks-last-confidence-institutions.aspx.

8. To read the data from Pew, see: http://www.pewresearch.org/fact-tank/2014/05/21/in-the-polls-tea-party-support-falls-among-republicans/.

9. To read the full results from People and the Press, see: http://www.people-press.org/2013/10/16/tea-partys-image-turns-more-negative/.

10. Parker and Barreto, *Change They Can't Believe In*.

11. Abramowitz, "Grand Old Tea Party."

12. Ibid.

13. Joseph Lowndes, "The Past and Future of Race in the Tea Party Movement," in *Steep: The Precipitous Rise of the Tea Party*, eds. Christine Trost and Lawrence Rosenthal (Berkeley: University of California Press, 2012), 171–192.

14. Parker and Barreto, *Change They Can't Believe In*.

15. The DREAM act, in all its forms, aims to provide a pathway to citizenship for children of undocumented residents of the country.

16. Parker and Barreto, *Change They Can't Believe In*, 165.

17. To read the full results from Pew, see: http://www.pewresearch.org/fact-tank/2014/06/11/tea-partiers-are-not-all-immigration-hawks/.

18. McBride, "Tax Fury and the Tea party," 303–324; Glenn Feldman, *The Irony of the Solid South: Democrats, Republicans, and Race, 1865–1944* (Tuscaloosa: University of Alabama Press, 2013).

19. To read the full data from IREHR, see: http://www.irehr.org/issue-areas/tea-party-nationalism/tea-party-news-and-analysis/item/527-status-of-tea-party-by-the-numbers.

20. McBride, "Tax Fury," 321.

21. Daniel Elazar, *American Federalism: A View from the South* (New York: Crowell, 1966).

22. Robert Erickson, John McIver, and John Wright, *Statehouse Democracy* (Cambridge, UK: Cambridge University Press, 1993).

23. McBride, "Tax Fury."

24. Stacy Ulbig and Sarah Macha, "It's Tea Time, but What Flavor? Regional Variation in Sources of Support for the Tea Party Movement," *American Review of Politics* 3, Summer (2012): 95–121.

25. Cari Lee Eastman, *Shaping the Immigration Debate: Contending Civic Societies on the US-Mexico Border* (Boulder, CO: First Forum Press/Lynne Rienner, 2012).

26. To read the full data from IREHR, see: http://www.irehr.org/issue-areas/tea-party-nationalism/beyond-fair-report/appendix-a-nativist-leaders-involved-in-tea-party-activity.

27. Ulbig and Macha, "It's Tea Time," 18.

28. Hans Noel, *Political Ideologies and Political Parties in America* (New York: Cambridge University Press, 2014): 185.

29. Ronald Rapoport, Meredith Dost, Ani-Rae Lovell, and Walter Stone, "Republican Factionalism and Tea Party Activists" (Presented at the Midwest Political Science Association Meeting Chicago, IL, 2012). http://wmpeople.wm.edu/asset/index/rbrapo/republicanfactionalismandteapartyactivists.

30. Ibid., 38.

31. Noel, *Political Ideologies and Political Parties in America*.

32. Gary Jacobson, "Partisan Media and Electoral Polarization 2012: Evidence from the American National Election Study" (Presented at the American Gridlock: Causes, Character, and Consequences, Washington, DC, 2014).

33. Kevin Arceneaux, and Martin Johnson, *Changing Minds or Changing Channels?: Partisan News in an Age of Choice* (Chicago: University of Chicago Press, 2012).

34. Aaron Blake, "Tea Party Democrats Do Exist," *The Washington Post*, July 5, 2011, http://www.washingtonpost.com/politics/tea-party-democrats-do-exist/2011/07/05/gHQAjeadzH_story.html.

35. Noel, *Political Ideologies and Political Parties in America*.

36. David Campbell, and Robert Putnam, "Crashing the Tea Party," *New York Times*, August 16, 2011, http://www.nytimes.com/2011/08/17/opinion/crashing-the-tea-party.html?_r=2&.

37. Ibid.

38. Joan Walsh, "Getting to Know the Tea Party," *Salon*, August 17, 2011, http://www.salon.com/2011/08/18/getting_to_know_the_tea_party/.

39. Peter Beinert, "Sam's Club Republicans vs. Tea Party," *Daily Beast*, October 29, 2013, http://www.thedailybeast.com/articles/2013/10/29/sam-s-club-republicans-vs-the-tea-party.html.

40. Kevin Arceneaux and Sean Nicholson, "Who Wants to Have a Tea Party: The Who, What, and Why of the Tea Party Movement," *PS* 45, no. 4 (2012): 700–710.

41. Ibid., 701.

42. Ibid., 704.

43. Ibid., 705.

44. David Kirby and Emily Ekins McClintock, "Libertarian Roots of the Tea Party" (Washington, DC: Cato Institute, August 6, 2012), http://www.cato.org/publications/policy-analysis/libertarian-roots-tea-party.

45. David Kirby, "More Data on Libertarian Roots of the Tea Party" (Washington, DC: Cato Institute, August 14, 2012), http://www.cato.org/publications/commentary/more-data-libertarian-roots-tea-party.

46. Melissa Deckman, "Mama Grizzlies and the Tea Party," in *Steep: The Precipitous Rise of the Tea Party*, eds. Christine Trost and Lawrence Rosenthal (Berkeley: University of California Press, 2012): 171–192.

47. Ibid.

48. Lee Mardsen, "Conservative Evangelicals, the Tea Party, and US Foreign Policy," in *Obama and the World: New Directions in US Foreign Policy*, eds. Inderjeet Parmar, Linda B. Miller, and Mark Ledwidge (New York: Routledge, 2014), 128.

49. Brian Rathbun, "Steeped in International Affairs: The Foreign Policy Views of the Tea Party," *Foreign Policy Analysis* 9, no. 1 (2011): 21–37.

50. To read the full results from the People and the Press poll, see: http://www.people-press.org/2011/10/07/strong-on-defense-and-israel-tough-on-china/.

51. Ibid.

CHAPTER 4

1. "'Countdown with Keith Olbermann' for Tuesday August 24, 2010," *NBCNews*, August 25, 2010, http://www.nbcnews.com/id/38848855/ns/msnbc-countdown_with_keith_olbermann/t/countdown-keith-olbermann-tuesday-august-th/#.U8Qu1kCty_c.

2. Skocpol and Williamson, *The Tea Party and the Remaking of Republican Conservatism*, 112.

3. Steven Teles, *The Rise of the Conservative Legal Movement* (Princeton, NJ: Princeton University Press, 2009).

4. Heath Brown, *Lobbying the New President: Interests in Transition* (New York: Routledge, 2012).

5. Phillip Mirowski, *Never Let a Serious Crisis Go to Waste* (New York: Verso, 2013).

6. Parker and Barreto, *Change They Can't Believe In*.

7. Amanda Fallin, Rachel Grana, and Stanton Glantz, "'To Quarterback behind the Scenes,' Third-Party Efforts: The Tobacco Industry and the Tea Party," *Tobacco Control* 2 (2013): 1–10.

8. Nicholas Carnes, *White-Collar Government: The Hidden Role of Class in Economic Policy Making* (Chicago: University of Chicago Press, 2013).

9. Ibid., 5

10. Ibid., 3.

11. Andrew Goldman, "The Billionaire's Party," *New York*, July 25, 2010, http://nymag.com/news/features/67285/.

12. Donald Abelson, *Do Think Tanks Matter: Assessing the Impact of Public Policy Institutes* (Quebec City, Canada: McGill-Queen's, 2002).

13. Andrew Selee, *What Should Think Tanks Do? A Strategic Guide to Policy Impact* (Stanford, CA: Stanford University Press, 2013).

14. To read Cato's full mission statement: see: http://www.cato.org/about.

15. To read the TPP vision statement, see: http://www.teapartypatriots.org/ourvision/.

16. To read the TPP mission statement, see: http://www.teapartyexpress.org/mission.

17. John Campbell and Ove Pedersen, *The National Origins of Policy Ideas: Knowledge Regimes in the United States, France, Germany, and Denmark* (Princeton, NJ: Princeton University Press, 2014).

18. Brown, *Lobbying the New President.*

19. Michael Scherer, "Inside Obama's Idea Factory in Washington," *Time: Online Edition*, November 21, 2008, http://www.time.com/time/politics/article/0,8599,1861305,00.html.

20. Kenneth Vogel, "Cato, Koch Brothers Settle Ownership Fight," *Politico*, June 25, 2012, http://www.politico.com/news/stories/0612/77809.html.

21. Jane Mayer, "Covert Operations: The Billionaire Brothers Who Are Waging a War against Obama," *The New Yorker*, August 20, 2010, http://www.newyorker.com/reporting/2010/08/30/100830fa_fact_mayer?currentPage=all.

22. Jane Mayer, "The Koch Brothers in California?" *The New Yorker*, August 25, 2013, http://www.newyorker.com/online/blogs/currency/2013/10/the-koch-brothers-in-california.html.

23. Jim Vandehei and Mike Allen, "Exclusive: The Koch Brothers' Secret Bank," *Politico*, September 11, 2013, http://www.politico.com/story/2013/09/behind-the-curtain-exclusive-the-koch-brothers-secret-bank-96669.html.

24. Michael Beckel, "Koch-Backed Nonprofit Spent Record Cash in 2012," The Center for Public Integrity, November 14, 2013, http://www.publicintegrity.org/2013/11/14/13712/koch-backed-nonprofit-spent-record-cash-2012.

25. Alan Pyke, "Astroturfing the Airwaves," Media Matters, October 25, 2010, http://politicalcorrection.org/blog/201010250007.

26. Matea Gold, "Koch-Backed Political Network Built to Shield Donors, Raised $400 Million in 2012 Elections," *The Washington Post*, January 5, 2013, http://www.washingtonpost.com/politics/koch-backed-political-network-built-to-shield-donors-raised-400-million-in-2012-elections/2014/01/05/9e7cfd9a-719b-11e3-9389-09ef9944065e_story.html.

27. Kim Phillips-Fein, "The Business Lobby and the Tea Party," *New Labor Forum* 2, no. 2 (2014): 14–19.

28. Michael Beckel, "Tea Party-Loving Republican Senate Candidates Propelled by Cash from Ideological Groups, Small Donors," Center for Responsive Politics, October 7, 2010, http://www.opensecrets.org/news/2010/10/tea-party-loving-republican-senate/.

29. Mike Allen, "Chamber Wary of 'Goofball' Candidates," *Politico*, May 21, 2014, http://www.politico.com/story/2014/05/chamber-wary-of-goofball-candidates-106980.html#ixzz37qOn3YVE.

30. Daniel Kreiss, *Taking Our Country Back: The Crafting of Networked Politics from Howard Dean to Barack Obama* (New York: Oxford University Press, 2012).

31. To learn more about Media Matters for America, see: http://mediamatters. org/.

32. Eric Hananoki, "'Fair and Balanced' Fox News Aggressively Promotes 'Tea Party' Protests," Media Matters, April 8, 2009, http://mediamatters.org/research/2009/04/08/report-fair-and-balanced-fox-news-aggressively/149009.

33. Skocpol and Williamson, *The Tea Party*.

34. Ibid., 132.

35. Julie Boykoff and Eulalie Laschever, "The Tea Party Movement, Framing, and US Media," *Social Movement Studies* 10, no. 4 (2011): 341–366.

36. The method of data collection relied on Lexis-Nexis through the Seton Hall University Library. Lexis-Nexis is a well-known database of a vast array of print, broadcast, and online news coverage. Using search functions, I could re-create the numbers of references to the Tea Party on each day from February 2009 to the summer of 2014. I set a conservative net for my data collection which focused on direct references to "Tea Party." I did not collect broader references to Freedom-Works, the Koch brothers, or other related people, organizations, and entities. I did this to prevent the daily counts of news stories to capture "false-positives" that mentioned one of the other terms, but did not directly focus on the Tea Party. In setting a conservative net, I also may have missed a small number of stories that did not directly mention "Tea Party" but were tangentially related. The counts reported in the graph then ·reflect a low-estimate, but one that likely correlates strongly and positive with broader data collection.

I collected data based on the transcripts made available through Lexis-Nexis. These transcripts provide a near verbatim recording of all of the verbal parts of major show segments broadcast each day. Skocpol and Williamson (2012) reported that CNN makes more transcripts available, potentially leading to the impression that their coverage is more extensive than other networks which provide fewer transcripts. For this reason, I opted to leave CNN out of the data analysis. Instead, I compared MSNBC and the Fox News Network, as these are natural competitors and seem to provide Lexis-Nexis with a similar amount of broadcast transcript data.

With the transcripts downloaded into Excel, I summed the number of segments that mentioned the Tea Party for each month. Monthly reports are small enough to observe changes in coverage, but not so small, such as daily, that my presentation of the data would be unclear. A limitation of this approach, though, is that we cannot pinpoint coverage on any particular day, rather each data point can be tracked to the month of an event, such as a rally or Election Day. I also did not distinguish between the intensity of focus on the Tea Party in each segment, meaning a single mention counts the same as an entire segment devoted to the subject. Given the focus of the analysis, this is a limitation that does not seem to greatly alter the findings.

37. Boykoff and Laschever, "The Tea Party Movement."

38. Anthony DiMaggio, *The Rise of the Tea Party: Political Discontent and Corporate Media in the Age of Obama* (New York: New York University Press, 2011): 111.

39. Damon DiCicco and Colin Lingle, "A Rising Tide of Tea and Ink: News Media Coverage of the Tea Party versus Other Major Protests" (Presented at APSA Political Communication Pre-Conference. Seattle, WA, 2011).

40. Ibid, 16.

41. David Weaver and Joseph Sacco, "Revisiting the Protest Paradigm: The Tea Party as Filtered through Prime-Time Cable News," *International Journal of Press/Politics* 18, no. 1 (2013): 61–84.

42. Amy Gardner, "The Tea Party and the Media," *The Washington Post*, October 27, 2010, http://www.washingtonpost.com/wp-dyn/content/article/2010/10/26/AR2010102606804.html.

43. Rachel Weiner, "Dick Armey Quits FreedomWorks," *The Washington Post*, December 3, 2012, http://www.washingtonpost.com/blogs/post-politics/wp/2012/12/03/dick-armey-quits-freedomworks/.

44. Andy Kroll, "Powerful Tea Party Group's Internal Docs Leak—Read Them Here," *Mother Jones*, January 4, 2013, http://www.motherjones.com/politics/2012/12/freedomworks-rich-donors-armey-kibbe-super-pac#update.

CHAPTER 5

1. Doug McAdam and Karina Kloos, *Deeply Divided: Racial Politics and Social Movements in Postwar America* (New York: Oxford University Press, 2014).

2. Davison M. Douglas, "The Rhetoric of Moderation: Desegregation in the South during the Decade after Brown," *Northwestern University Law Review* 89, no. 1 (1994): 92–139.

3. Michael Heaney and Fabio Rojas, *Party in the Street: The Antiwar Movement and the Democratic Party after 9/11* (New York: Cambridge University Press, 2015).

4. Jonathan Mummolo, "Nimble Giants: How National Interest Groups Harnessed Tea Party Enthusiasm," in *Interest Groups Unleashed*, eds. Paul Herrnson, Christopher Deering, and Clyde Wilcox (Thousand Oaks, CA: Sage Publishers, 2013): 193–212.

5. Josh Kraushaar, "Rep. Labrador Wins Idaho Primary Upset," *Politico*, May 26, 2010, http://www.politico.com/news/stories/0510/37790.html.

6. "Tea Party Boise Endorses Raul Labrador," KTVB, November 24, 2013, http://www.ktvb.com/story/local/2015/03/30/11518079/.

7. Jason Breslow, "In Their Own Words: The GOP's 2010 Freshmen and the Politics of Debt," PBS Frontline, February 12, 2013, http://www.pbs.org/wgbh/pages/frontline/government-elections-politics/cliffhanger/in-their-own-words-the-gops-2010-freshmen-and-the-politics-of-debt/.

8. James Rowley, "Puerto Rico-Born Labrador Top Republican on Immigration," *Bloomberg*, April 5, 2013, http://www.bloomberg.com/news/articles/2013-04-05/puerto-rico-born-labrador-top-republican-on-immigration.

9. Robert Koenig, "Iron Lady or Mama Grizzly?" *St. Louis Beacon*, November 9, 2010, https://www.stlbeacon.org/#!/content/17652/introducing_vicky_hartzler.

10. To read the polling from the race, see: http://www.realclearpolitics.com/epolls/2010/house/mo/missouri_4th_district_hartzler_vs_skelton-1292.html.

11. To read the electoral map, see: http://www.nytimes.com/interactive/2010/11/04/us/politics/tea-party-results.html?ref=politics&_r=0.

12. Dhrumil Mehta, "The Age of Tea Party Members in Congress," *FiveThirtyEight*, May 5, 2014, http://fivethirtyeight.com/datalab/the-age-of-tea-party-members-in-congress/.

13. Nicholas Carnes, *White Collar Government* (Chicago: University of Chicago Press, 2013).

14. Seth Cline, "Tea Party House Members Even Wealthier than Other GOP Lawmakers," Center for Responsive Politics, January 4, 2012, http://www.opensecrets.org/news/2012/01/tea-party-house-members-wealthy-gop/.

15. See http://www.clubforgrowth.org/about/.

16. Binyamin Applebaum and Jennifer Steinhauer, "Congress Ends 5-Year Standoff on Trade Deals in Rare Accord," *New York Times*, October 21, 2011, http://www.nytimes.com/2011/10/13/business/trade-bills-near-final-chapter.html?pagewanted=all.

17. For the full press release, see http://mckinley.house.gov/s2011/mckinley-votes-against-trade-deals/.

18. Jesse Rhodes, *An Education in Politics: The Origin and Evolution of No Child Left Behind* (Ithaca, NY: Cornell University Press, 2012).

19. Alyson Klein, "Congress Chops Funding for High-Profile Education Programs," *Education Week*, March 9, 2011, http://www.edweek.org/ew/articles/2011/03/04/23fedbudget.html?tkn=VVYFCK0gQBZuF2hCKUhgoqSLts2ElQWpUfE3&cmp=clp-edweek.

20. Caitlin McDevitt, "Matt Damon Weighs in on the Debt Ceiling," *Politico*, August 1, 2011, http://www.politico.com/blogs/click/0811/Matt_Damon_weighs_in_on_the_debt_ceiling.html.

21. Raul Labrador and Mike Pompeo, "Era of Energy Subsidies Is Over," *The Washington Times*, November 26, 2011, http://www.washingtontimes.com/news/2011/nov/26/era-of-energy-subsidies-is-over/#ixzz3HjqOuGok.

22. Rob Hotokainen, "Congress Divided over Continuing Subsidization of Wind Power," McClatchyDC, November 14, 2011, http://www.mcclatchydc.com/2011/11/14/130279/congress-divided-over-continuing.html.

23. Anthony Leiserowitz, Edward Mailbach, Connie Roser-Renouf, and Jay Hmielowski, "Politics & Global Warming: Democrats, Republicans, Independents and the Tea Party," Yale Project on Climate Change Communication, May 12, 2011, http://environment.yale.edu/climate/files/PoliticsGlobalWarming2011.pdf.

24. Wes Barrett, "Tea Party Slams Boehner and Ryan on Debt Ceiling," *FoxNews*, May 9, 2011, http://www.foxnews.com/politics/2011/05/09/tea-party-slams-boehner-and-ryan-on-debt-ceiling/.

25. Breslow, "In Their Own Words."

26. To read the full statement made by Congressman Amash, see: https://amash.house.gov/press-release/amash-issues-statement-after-house-debt-vote.

27. To read the full statement, see: http://mckinley.house.gov/common/popup/popup.cfm?action=item.print&itemID=185.

28. Andreas Madestam, Daniel Shoag, Stan Veuger, and David Yanagizawa-Drott, "Do Political Protests Matter? Evidence from the Tea Party Movement," *Economic Policy Working Paper* (Washington, DC: American Enterprise Institute, 2013).

29. To read the full results from the poll, see: http://www.people-press.org/2011/11/29/more-now-disagree-with-tea-party-even-in-tea-party-districts/.

30. Ezra Klein, "People Don't Fully Appreciate How Committed the Tea Party Is to Not Compromising," *The Washington Post*, October 4, 2013, http://www.washingtonpost.com/blogs/wonkblog/wp/2013/10/04/people-dont-fully-appreciate-how-committed-the-tea-party-is-to-not-compromising/.

31. Douglas Blackmon and Jennifer Levitz, "Tea Party Sees No Triumph in Compromise," *The Wall Street Journal*, October 2, 2011, http://online.wsj.com/news/articles/SB10001424053111903635604576474050402040650.

32. In 2014, Tea Party organizations endorsed 80 candidates and nearly three-quarters (73%) won. Devin Burghart, "Tea Party Endorsed Candidates Dominate," IREHR, November 5, 2014, http://www.irehr.org/issue-areas/tea-party-nationalism/tea-party-news-and-analysis/610-tea-party-election-2014.

33. Ion Bogdan Vasi, David Strang, and Arnout van de Rijt, "Tea and Sympathy: The Tea Party Movement and Republican Precommitment to Radical Conservatism in the 2011 Debt-Limit Crisis," *Mobilization: An International Quarterly* 19, no. 1 (2014): 1–22.

CHAPTER 6

1. Devin Burghart, "Tea Party Endorsed Candidates Dominate," IREHR, November 5, 2014, http://www.irehr.org/issue-areas/tea-party-nationalism/tea-party-news-and-analysis/610-tea-party-election-2014.

2. To read the full data, see: https://www.opensecrets.org/pres08/.

3. Mark Leibovich, "The First Senator from the Tea Party?" *New York Times Magazine*, January 4, 2010: MM29, http://www.nytimes.com/2010/01/10/magazine/10florida-t.html?pagewanted=all&_r=0.

4. Annie Gowen, "Marco Rubio, from Exile to Tea Party Hero," *The Washington Post*, November 4, 2010: A1, http://www.washingtonpost.com/wp-dyn/content/article/2010/11/03/AR2010110308200.html.

5. Peter Montgomery, "The Tea Party and Religious Right Movements: Frenemies with Benefits," in *Steep: The Precipitous Rise of the Tea Party*, ed. Christine Trost and Lawrence Rosenthal (Berkeley, CA: University of California Press, 2012), 242–274.

6. To see all of the interest group rankings of Senator Rubio, see: http://votesmart.org/candidate/evaluations/1601/marco-rubio#.U9exXqMveAQ.

7. Alex Pappas, "Survey: Marco Rubio Is the Tea Party Choice for Vice President," *Daily Caller*, July 18, 2012, http://dailycaller.com/2012/07/18/survey-marco-rubio-is-the-tea-party-choice-for-vice-president/.

8. To read the full statement by Senator Rubio, see: http://www.rubio.senate.gov/public/index.cfm/press-releases?ID=85a7f16e-7b91-4f44-8c68-129ebd25a865.

9. Dana Milbank, "Tea Party Scalds Marco Rubio," *The Washington Post*, June 19, 2013, http://www.washingtonpost.com/opinions/dana-milbank-tea-party-scalds-marco-rubio/2013/06/19/468e6926-d924-11e2-a9f2-42ee3912ae0e_story.html.

10. To read the full Quinnipiac poll results, see: http://www.quinnipiac.edu/news-and-events/quinnipiac-university-poll/florida/release-detail?ReleaseID=1910.

11. Paige Lavender, "Sarah Palin: 'I'll Never Say Never' to a 2016 Presidential Run," *Huffington Post*, March 3, 2014, http://www.huffingtonpost.com/2014/03/10/sarah-palin-2016_n_4934072.html.

12. To read the full poll results, see: http://www.targetpointconsulting.com/system/uploads/22/original/POLITICO-TargetPoint_Tea_Party_Exit_Poll_Findings.pdf?1271686652.

13. To read the full Tea Party Express statement, see: http://www.teapartyexpress.org/7119/governor-sarah-palin-to-attend-tea-party-express-rally.

14. To read all of the endorsements made by Sarah Palin, see: http://www.washingtonpost.com/wp-srv/special/politics/palin_tracker/.

15. Jeff Poor, "Sarah Paling: Primary Marco Rubio, Kelly Ayotte," *The Daily Caller*, June 26, 2013, http://dailycaller.com/2013/06/26/sarah-palin-primary-marco-rubio-kelly-ayotte/.

16. Emily Ekins, "Ron Paul Rising: Evidence from National Polls on Ron Paul's Supporters," *Reason.Com*, January 13, 2012, http://reason.com/poll/2012/01/13/ron-paul-rising-evidenc-from-national-po.

17. Rand Paul, "Sen. Rand Paul: My Filibuster Was Just the Beginning," *The Washington Post*, March 8, 2013, http://www.washingtonpost.com/opinions/sen-rand-paul-my-filibuster-was-just-the-beginning/2013/03/08/6352d8a8-881b-11e2-9d71-f0feafdd1394_story.html.

18. "CNN Poll: Rand Paul Goes Where His Father Never Went," CNN, March 3, 2014, http://politicalticker.blogs.cnn.com/2014/03/16/cnn-poll-rand-paul-goes-where-his-father-never-went/.

19. Aaron Blake, "Rand Paul Is Right Where He Wants for the 2016 Race," *The Washington Post*, July 17, 2014, http://www.washingtonpost.com/blogs/the-fix/wp/2014/07/17/rand-paul-is-right-where-he-wants-to-be-in-the-2016-race/

20. Eric Heberlig and Bruce Larson, *Congressional Parties, Institutional Ambition and the Financing of Congressional Parties* (Ann Arbor: University of Michigan Press, 2012).

21. For the full data on Sarah PAC, see: https://www.opensecrets.org/pacs/lookup2.php?strID=C00458588&cycle=2010.

22. To read the data, see: https://www.opensecrets.org/politicians/summary.php?cid=N00030612&cycle=2014.

23. In order to analyze news coverage, I conducted separate searches using Lexis-Nexis. I then counted the number of times the names "Sarah Palin," "Rand Paul," and "Marco Rubio" appeared on transcripts for Fox News Network and MSNBC. I did these counts for each month from January 2009, until July 2014.

24. Matthew Corrigan, *Conservative Hurricane: How Jeb Bush Remade* (Gainesville: University Press of Florida, 2014).

25. Kristin Goss, *The Paradox of Gender Equality: How American Women's Groups Gained and Lost Their Public Voice* (Ann Arbor: University of Michigan Press, 2013), 72.

26. Noel, *Political Ideologies and Political Parties in America*, 176.

27. For read more about the Export-Import Bank, see: http://www.exim.gov/about/.

28. "Crony Capitalism and Your Tax Dollars: The Export-Import Bank," Tea Party Patriots April 11, 2013, http://www.teapartypatriots.org/all-issues/news/crony-capitalism-and-your-tax-dollars-the-export-import-bank/.

29. For more information, see: http://www.exim.gov/newsandevents/the-facts-about-ex-im-bank.cfm.

30. Zachary Goldfarb and Holly Yeager, "Long-Building Conservative Anger at Export-Import Bank Reaches Boiling Point," *The Washington Post*, June 28, 2014, http://www.washingtonpost.com/business/economy/long-building-conservative-anger-at-export-import-bank-reaches-boiling-point/2014/06/27/cce4a87a-fe01-11e3-b1f4-8e77c632c07b_story.html.

31. To read the full data from the Gallup poll, see: http://www.gallup.com/poll/152096/americans-anti-big-business-big-gov.aspx.

32. To read about the Common Core Standards, see: http://www.corestandards.org/about-the-standards/.

33. Motoko Rich, "Common Core School Standards Face a New Wave of Opposition," *New York Times*, May 28, 2014, http://www.nytimes.com/2014/05/30/education/common-core-standards-face-a-new-wave-of-opposition.html.

34. To read the full mission statement for the Columbia Tea Party, see: http://columbiateaparty.org/our-mission/faqs/.

35. Patrik Jonsson, "Republicans Getting Buzzed on Pot Possibilities?" *The Christian Science Monitor*, May 31, 2014, http://www.csmonitor.com/USA/Politics/2014/0531/Republicans-getting-buzzed-on-pot-possibilities-video.

36. To read the full poll results from Reason, see: http://reason.com/poll/2012/11/14/73-percent-of-americans-think-medical-ma.

37. To read the full poll results, see: http://www.people-press.org/2013/04/04/majority-now-supports-legalizing-marijuana/.

38. John Hudak, "Bipartisanship: Brought to You by the Tea Party," *The Hill*, June 10, 2014, http://thehill.com/blogs/pundits-blog/208492-bipartisanship-brought-to-you-by-the-tea-party.

39. Lucia Graves, "Rand Paul's Quiet Weed Overture," *National Journal*, July 25, 2014, http://www.nationaljournal.com/politics/rand-paul-s-quiet-weed-overture-20140725.

40. Aaron Gould Sheinin, "Tea Party Leader Backs Medical Marijuana Bill," *The Atlanta Journal-Constitution*, February 2, 2014, http://www.ajc.com/news/news/tea-party-leader-backs-medical-marijuana-bill/ndJt4/.

41. Evan Halper, "Why Republicans Are Slowly Embracing Marijuana," *The Los Angeles Times*, May 30, 2014, http://www.latimes.com/nation/politics/politicsnow/la-pn-gop-marijuana-20140530-story.html.

Index

The letter "f" indicates material in figures. The letter "n" indicates material in endnotes. The letter "t" indicates material in tables.

About the Author

HEATH BROWN, PhD, is assistant professor of public policy at John Jay College of Criminal Justice, City University of New York, New York. He has previously published *Lobbying the New President: Interest in Transition*.